MERMAID SAGA

2

Story and Art by

Rumiko Takahashi

CONTENTS

Chapter 10
Mermaid's Scar, Part 1
7

Chapter 11
Mermaid's Scar, Part 2
59

Chapter 12
The Ash Princess
111

Chapter 13
Mermaid's Gaze, Part 1
175

Chapter 14
Mermaid's Gaze, Part 2
227

Chapter 15
Mermaid's Mask, Part 1
277

Chapter 16
Mermaid's Mask, Part 2
317

PTUM PTUM PTUM
YOU CAME ALL THE WAY FROM TOKYO BY YOURSELF?
THAT'S IMPRESSIVE.
I CAME TO SEE MY MOMMY.
FROM NOW ON WE'RE GOING TO LIVE TOGETHER.
AH! THAT'S MY MOMMY THERE.
PSHAAA

SHING SHING
MOMMY!
PTUM PTUM
PTUM PTUM

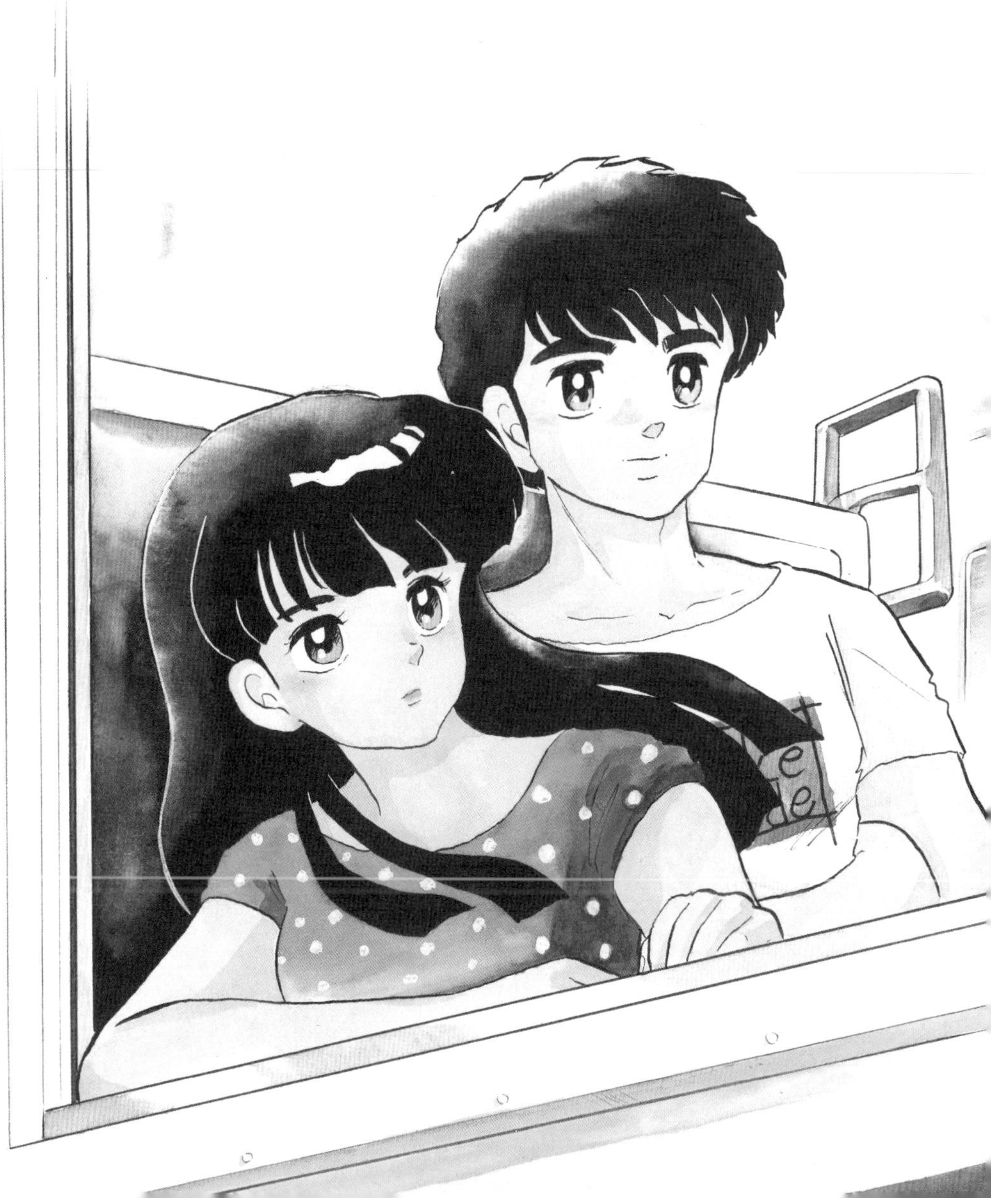

Chapter 10: Mermaid's Scar, Part 1

TWO YEARS LATER ...
FWOOOOOOO
KREE
KREE

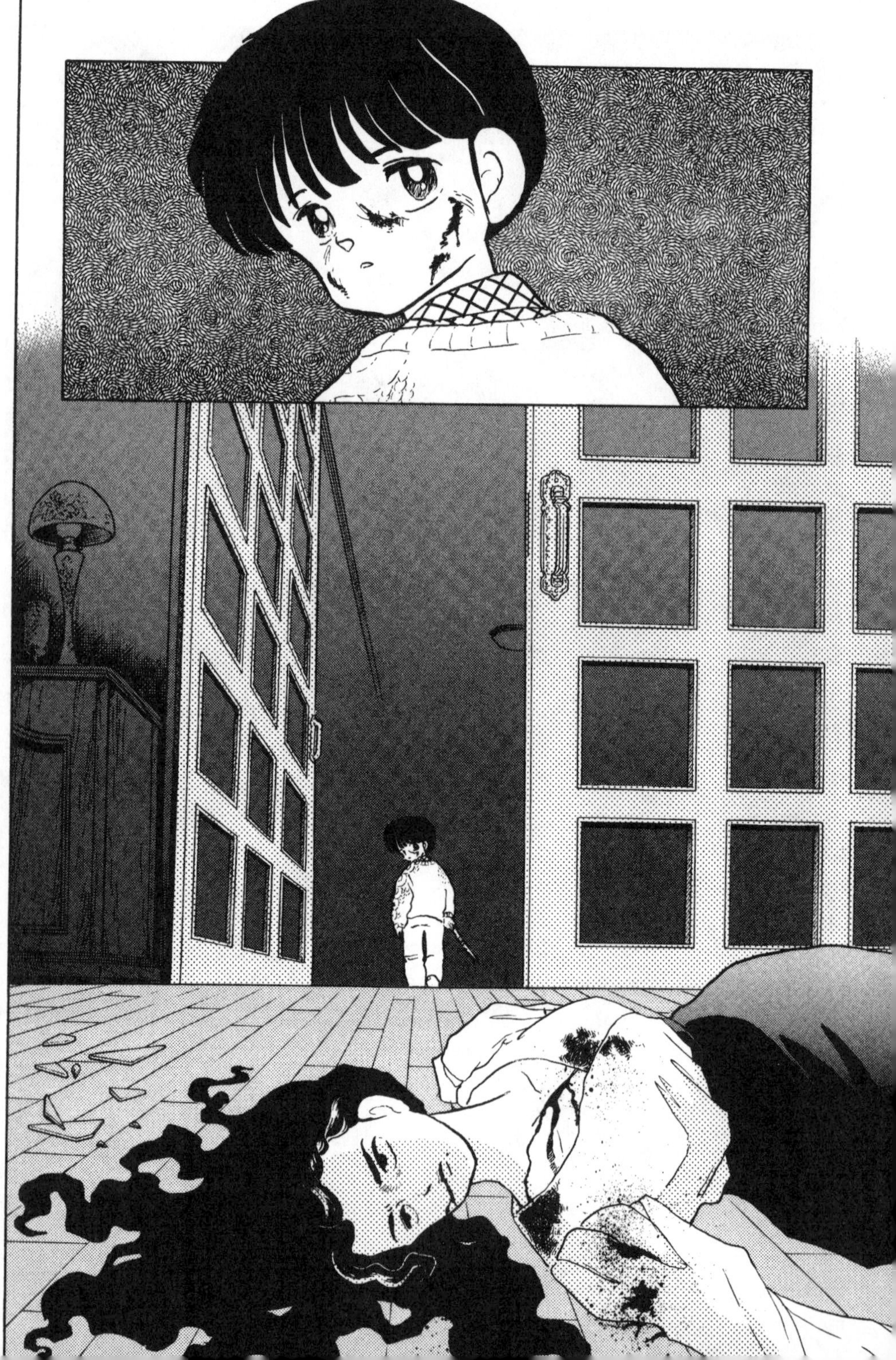

SPLASH
SWSH
SWSH
SWSH
SHAAAA
SPLSH
SPLSH

MOMMY...

KLANK
GOOD MORNING!
HI, YUKIE.
TMP
HELLO, MASATO.
WHERE'S YOUR MOTHER?
TMP
SHE'S ...
...STILL ASLEEP.

GOOD MORN-ING.
MASATO ...
OH, GOOD MORNING, MA'AM.
!
HM?
FWSH
MASATO. COME TO MOMMY.
CLUTCH
...

KLANK
KLANK
THE STORY ABOUT THE MONSTER THAT WAS FLOATING IN THE OCEAN?
OH SURE.
I GUESS IT WAS JUST ABOUT A YEAR AGO.
A WEIRD CORPSE WAS BOBBING IN THE WATER BY THE WHARF.
YOU SAW IT?

I COULD SEE ARMS AND LEGS LIKE A HUMAN'S ...
...BUT IT HAD A REAL GRUESOME FACE, LIKE A FISH'S.
THEN IT GOT SWALLOWED UP IN THE WAVES AND DISAPPEARED.
WE STILL DON'T KNOW WHAT THE HELL IT WAS.
...
BANG BANG BANG
POP
fun tea

HAVEN'T YOU EVER MADE TEA BEFORE?!
FOR CRYING OUT LOUD!
CAN SAVE YOUR LIFE
AHHH-HHH!
GLUB GLUB GLUB GLUB
fun tea
WHAT'S THE MATTER WITH THIS CHILD?!
YUTA.
WHAT DID YOU DO THIS TIME?
MANA ...
WHY, HELLO, YUKIE.
HI, MRS. SUZUKI.
I'M SORRY. SHE'S LED A VERY SHELTERED LIFE.
SHE GETS ANGRY SO EASILY.
HMPH! IT'S NOT LIKE SHE'S A PRINCESS!
fun tea

WE WERE ON OUR WAY HOME FROM SHOPPING...
...AND THOUGHT WE'D STOP BY.
YOU MART
AH! NOW WOULD THIS BE...
...THE YOUNG MASTER FROM THE MANSION?
...
A PLACE FOR EVERYTHING AND EVERYTHING IN ITS PLACE.
YUTA, THAT LITTLE BOY...
HM?
WHAT ABOUT HIM?
REMEMBER WHEN I RODE ON A TRAIN FOR THE FIRST TIME?

NOT THAT YOU'D REMEMBER. IT WAS A LONG TIME AGO.
YOU TWO KNOW EACH OTHER?
HM?
OHHH, YEAH. YOU'RE THAT KID.
STILL A SQUIRT, AREN'T YOU?
AH...
YOU WERE TELLING US ABOUT COMING TO SEE YOUR MOTHER.
I DON'T THINK HIS MOTHER HAS LOOKED INTO IT YET.
YUKIE, ISN'T THAT BOY IN SCHOOL?
WSP WSP
ACTUALLY, I'M KIND OF SCARED OF HER.
YEAH.
...
ARE YOU HAPPY HERE?

THERE ARE SOME STRANGE RUMORS...
...ABOUT THE MISTRESS OF THE HOUSE YUKIE WORKS AT.
HM?
SHE'S THE SECOND WIFE OF A RICH OLD MAN.
TWO OR THREE YEARS AGO...
A MOM
CAUT
CAN S
...WHILE THEY WERE OUT ON THEIR YACHT...
...THEY CRASHED WITH A MOTOR-BOAT.
THE HUSBAND DIED.
SHE WAS SUPPOSED TO BE DEAD TOO. APPARENTLY SHE WAS HORRIBLY BURNED OVER HER WHOLE BODY.
BUT THEN, RUMOR HAS IT SHE CAME BACK TO LIFE!

TO TOP IT OFF, THE NEXT DAY SHE DISAPPEARED FROM THE HOSPITAL.
WHEN SHE RETURNED TO THE HOUSE SOME TIME LATER, SHE WAS JUST AS SHE HAD BEEN BEFORE THE ACCIDENT.
ONE OF THE MAIDS WHO HAD SEEN HER IN THE HOSPITAL...
...SAID THERE WAS NO WAY SHE COULD HAVE HEALED IN THAT SPACE OF TIME.
A WOMAN WHO CAME BACK TO LIFE...
A WEIRD CORPSE IN THE WATER...

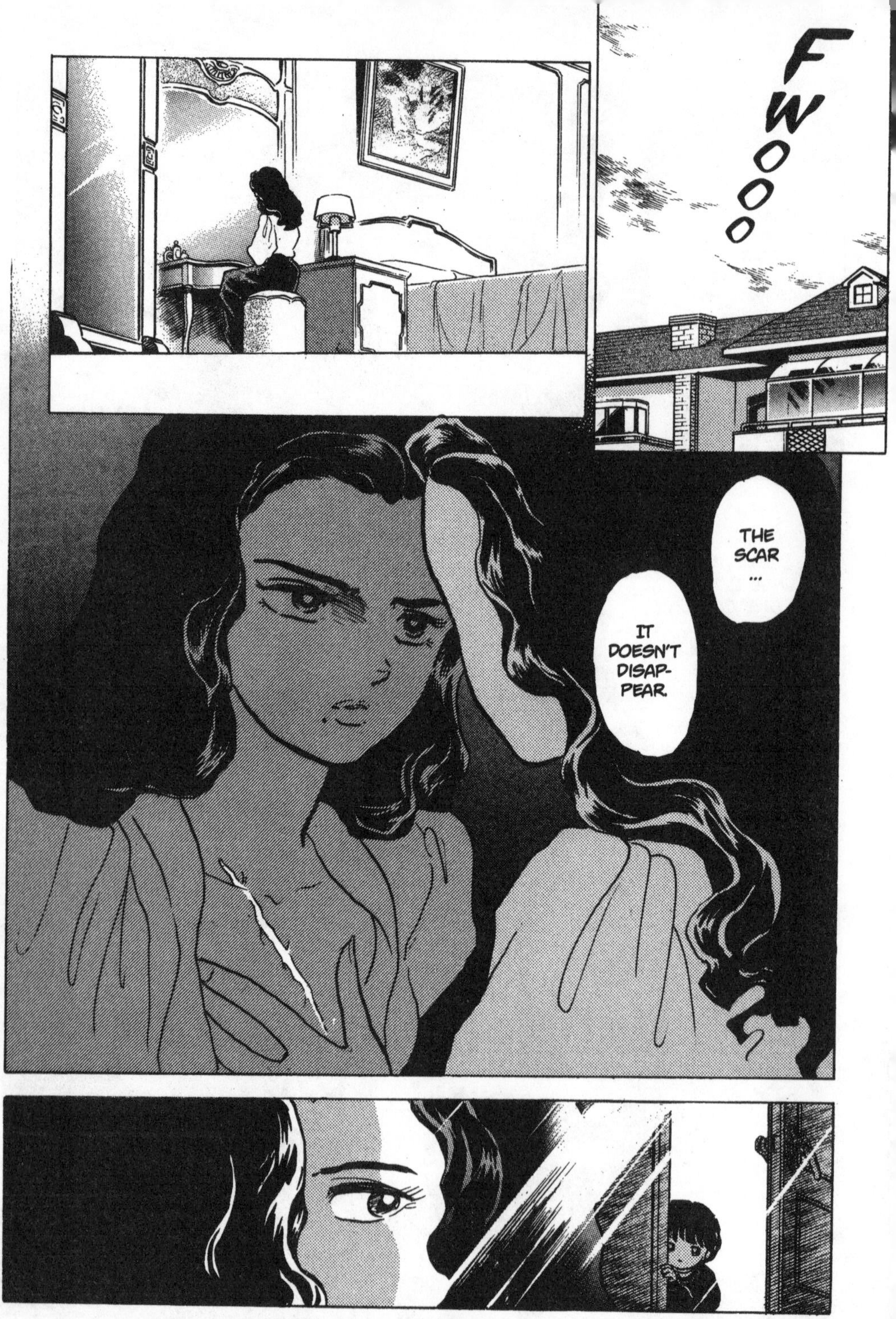
FWOOOO
THE SCAR ...
IT DOESN'T DISAP-PEAR.

SHUP
TWITCH
TMP TMP TMP TMP
CHAK
AH!

WHERE DID YOU HIDE THE MERMAID FLESH?!
I DON'T KNOW!
I DON'T KNOW!
MA'AM !!
DASH
GRAB
SHK

WHAT THE HELL IS THIS ABOUT?
...
...
FLUMP

FWOOOO
THERE YOU GO.
THE CUT WASN'T AS BAD AS I THOUGHT.
YUTA, WAS IT?
I'M SO GLAD YOU SHOWED UP WHEN YOU DID.
WHAT ABOUT HIS MOTHER?
SHE SEEMS TO HAVE CALMED DOWN.
WHAT SHOULD I DO? CALL THE POLICE?
NO!
I DON'T WANT MOMMY TO BE ARRESTED.
PLEASE DON'T TELL ANYONE WHAT HAPPENED.

YUTA ...?
I'M GOING TO TALK WITH HIS MOTHER ...
...AND TELL HER NOT TO BEAT UP ON THE KID.
...
KNOCK KNOCK
I CAME TO SEE YOU.
WHO ARE YOU?
SWISH

NOT BAD, HUH?
YOU ...
I ATE THE FLESH OF A MERMAID.
I'VE BEEN ALIVE 500 YEARS.
MOST WOUNDS HEAL UP RIGHT AWAY...
...BUT EVEN IF I DIE, I COME BACK TO LIFE BEFORE HALF A DAY IS OUT.
YOU ATE IT TOO, DIDN'T YOU?
AND I'LL BET YOU HAVE SOME MERMAID FLESH EVEN NOW.
!
HOW DID YOU-?!
THAT MONSTER THEY SAY FLOATED UP AT THE WHARF LAST YEAR...

I'LL BET THAT WAS A LOST SOUL...
...SOME-ONE WHO ATE THE FLESH OF A MERMAID BUT DIDN'T BECOME IMMORTAL.
MERMAID FLESH IS A VIOLENT POISON.
MOST PEOPLE EITHER DIE...
...OR BECOME MONSTERS.
IF WHAT YOU SAY IS TRUE...
MOMMY ...

WHAT'S WRONG, MOMMY?
WHAT'S MERMAID FLESH?
...
...
SWSH
WE'LL TALK AGAIN WHEN THE BOY ISN'T AROUND.
ARE YOU SURE YOU'RE ALL RIGHT, MASATO?
WOULD YOU LIKE ME TO STAY THE NIGHT?
WELL, THEN, HOW ABOUT COMING WITH ME?
IT'S JUST A BUNK-HOUSE, BUT...
NO.
IT'S OKAY NOW.
THAT BOY...
I'VE GOT TO HELP HIM SOMEHOW.

MERMAID FLESH IS A POISON?
NOT EVERYONE WHO EATS IT GAINS IMMORTALITY?
DOES THAT MEAN I MIGHT DIE SOMEDAY?
I'VE GOT TO FIND IT.
I'VE GOT TO FIND THE MERMAID FLESH BEFORE I DIE!
SHA
KLANG
KLANG
BAM BAM
BAM BAM
YOU'RE QUITTING YOUR JOB, YUKIE?
YES.

OOH!
WHAT A PRETTY RING.
WHAT?!
SO IT'S OFFICIAL NOW, IS IT?
CON-GRATU-LATIONS.
YES.
HE FINALLY ASKED ME.
IS THAT SO?
WELL, I'M VERY HAPPY FOR YOU.
I WISH I COULD HAVE DONE MORE FOR MASATO.
I FEEL LIKE I'M RUNNING OUT ON HIM.
YOU REALLY ARE A GOOD PERSON, AREN'T YOU?
YOU'LL MAKE A GOOD WIFE.
THANKS.
WELL...
SO LONG!

"ONE OF US" ...?
YOU MEAN THAT WOMAN WHO CAME BACK TO LIFE?
WELL ...
SHE DOESN'T SEEM LIKE THE EASIEST PERSON TO DEAL WITH.
ARE WE GOING TO TAKE HER WITH US?
SOMEHOW, I DON'T THINK SHE'D BE INTO THAT.
ANYWAY...
WE CAN'T JUST LEAVE THE BOY IN THAT SITUATION.
I SEE.
SO YOU WON'T BE WORKING WITH US ANYMORE.

WELL, I'M GLAD FOR YOU.
I'M SURE YOU'LL BE VERY HAPPY.
TH...
THANK YOU VERY MUCH.
TMP TMP
MASATO!
MASATO, WHERE ARE YOU?
MASATO?
YOU'RE QUIT-TING ...
...AREN'T YOU, YUKIE?
AH...
YOU WERE LISTEN-ING?

I'M SORRY.
I WISH I COULD HAVE STAYED WITH YOU LONGER.
YUKIE.
TRY THIS.
HM?
WHAT'S THIS?

SHA
B-DMP
?
!
KRASH
TMP

DASH
TMP TMP TMP TMP
MASA-TO!!
SHAK
!

VSSH
AHHH!

WHA-?!

IT'S A LOST SOUL.
VSH
AHHHH!
FWUMP
TMP TMP TMP TMP
DASH

TMP TMP TMP TMP TMP
SHUNK
WHAK
MANA!
TAKE THE BOY AND RUN!!
GRAB
GET UP!!

UNH...
SHAAK
YOU'RE NOT GETTING AWAY FROM ME!
AHHH!
CHOMP

WHA-?!
WHAT ARE YOU DOING?!
SHOVE
DAMN YOU ...
DAMN YOU!!
TMP TMP TMP TMP
HFF...
HFF...
SHA

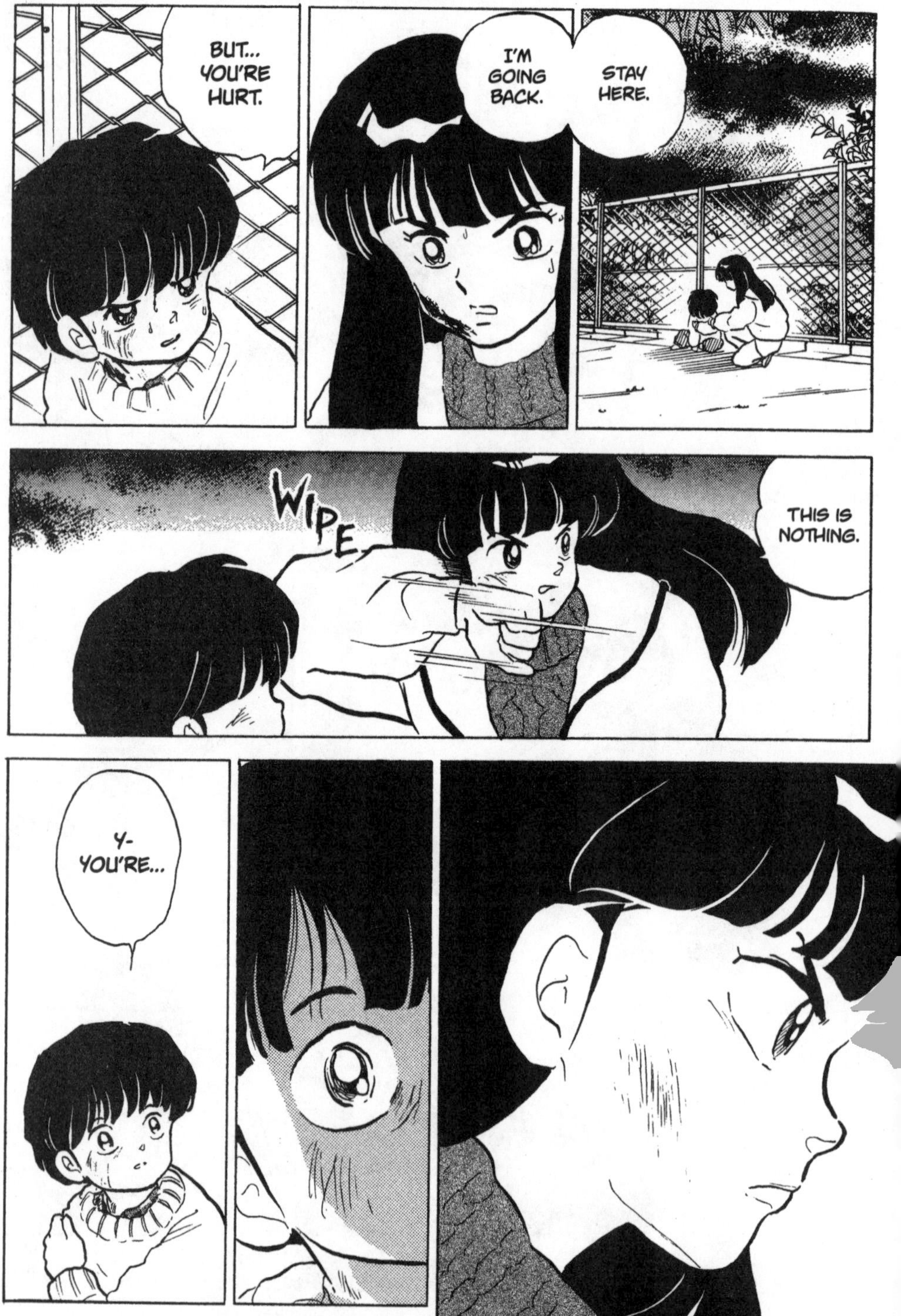
BUT... YOU'RE HURT.
I'M GOING BACK.
STAY HERE.
WIPE
THIS IS NOTHING.
Y- YOU'RE...

HFF...
HFF...
HFF...
HISSS
SHK
FWUNK

STAGGER
BAM
UNGH!
GRNCH
SKSH
FLUMP
TUMP
PHEW
UNH...
GLISH
...

TINK
YUKIE...

NHN...
YOU!!
WHAT THE HELL IS THIS ABOUT?!
AN-SWER ME!
WHY YUKIE?!
D-DAMN HIM.
HE...
HE TRIED TO REPLACE ME...
DON'T LET HIM FOOL YOU.
THE FIRST TIME... I MET MASATO...

!
THE DAY AFTER THE HEAVIEST BOMBING TOKYO HAD EVER SEEN.
...WAS DURING WORLD WAR II ...
MY ONLY SON, BARELY EIGHT YEARS OLD, HAD DIED IN THE BOMBING.
MY HUSBAND HAD LONG SINCE DIED IN BATTLE.
I HAD LOST THE WILL TO LIVE...
I WAS ALONE IN THE WORLD.
IT WAS JUST THEN...
...THAT HE APPEARED.
FSH

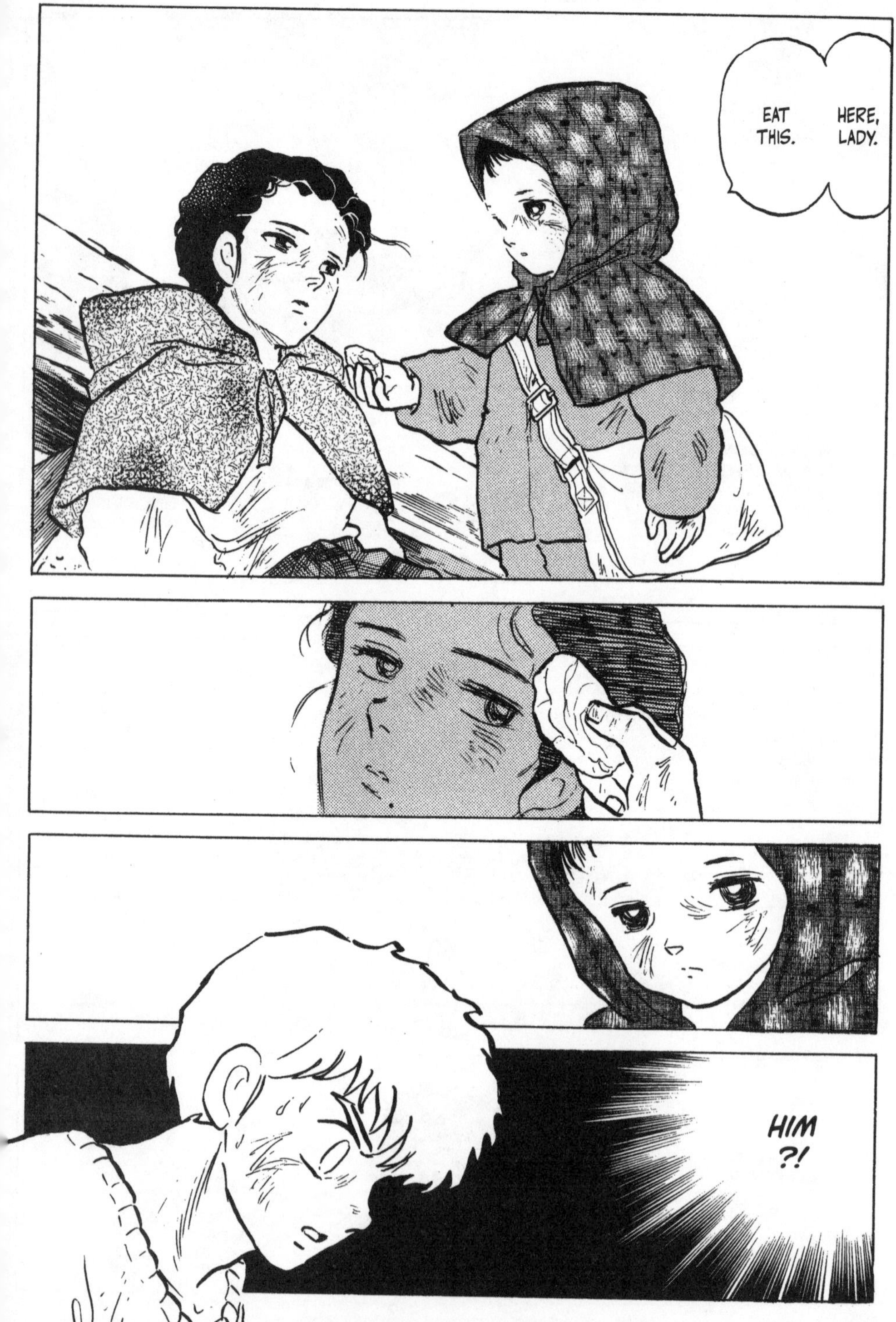
HERE, LADY.
EAT THIS.
HIM ?!

AFTER THAT...
...HE JUST BEGAN TO TAKE CARE OF ME, NEVER ASKING ME FOR ANYTHING.
AND I...
I FELT ALMOST AS IF MY DEAD SON HAD COME BACK TO ME.
WE BEGAN TO LIVE JUST AS IF WE WERE MOTHER AND CHILD.
BUT...
NO MATTER HOW MANY YEARS PASSED, HE NEVER GREW.
AND WHEN I INJURED MYSELF, THE WOUNDS WOULD HEAL SO QUICKLY YOU COULD WATCH IT HAPPENING.
I WAS AFRAID.
JUST WHAT ARE YOU?
HE TOLD ME THAT LONG AGO HE ATE THE FLESH OF A MERMAID. AND HE HAD GIVEN THE SAME TO ME.
BEING WITH A CHILD WHO NEVER GREW...
I COULDN'T STAY IN THE SAME PLACE FOR THREE YEARS.
ONCE, AT A LOSS FOR WHAT TO DO, I STRANGLED HIM.
BUT HE CAME BACK TO LIFE.

I RAN AWAY FROM HIM AND GOT MARRIED.
BUT JUST AS I WAS FINALLY BEGINNING TO LEAD A NORMAL LIFE...
HE MUST HAVE READ ABOUT THE YACHT ACCIDENT IN THE NEWSPAPER.
HE CAME AFTER ME.
MOMMY!
AS LONG AS I LIVE... I'LL NEVER ESCAPE HIM.
BUT LATELY...
...MY WOUNDS ...
...HAVEN'T HEALED AS QUICKLY AS THEY USED TO.
WHEN I TOLD HIM, HE JUST SAID...
THAT'S OKAY.
I'LL JUST LOOK FOR SOMEONE TO TAKE YOUR PLACE.
IF WE DON'T GET THE MERMAID FLESH AWAY FROM HIM...
...HE'LL DO IT AGAIN... AND AGAIN ...

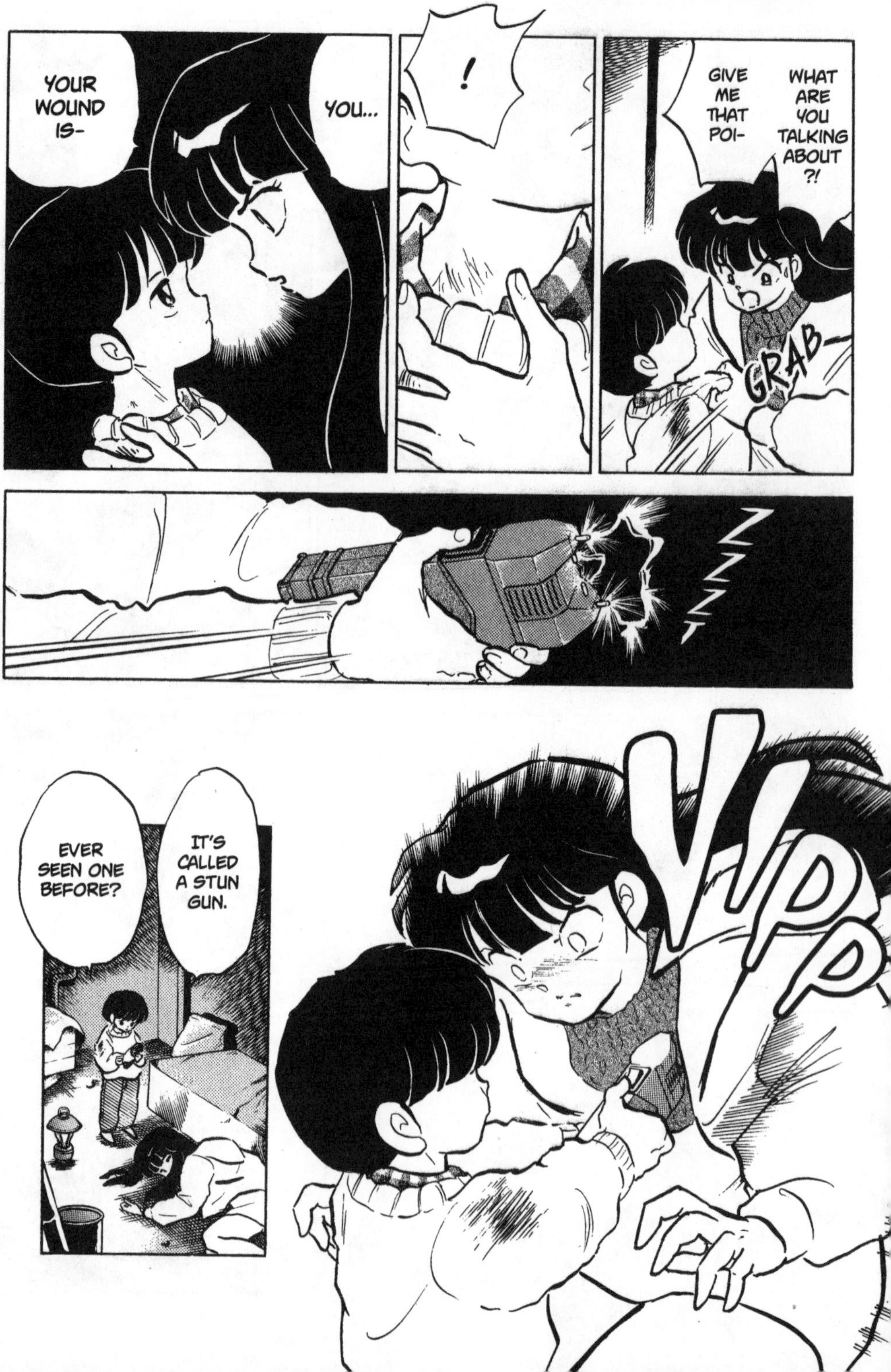
WHAT ARE YOU TALKING ABOUT?!
GIVE ME THAT POI-
GRAB
!
YOU...
YOUR WOUND IS-
ZZZZZT
VIPP
IT'S CALLED A STUN GUN.
EVER SEEN ONE BEFORE?

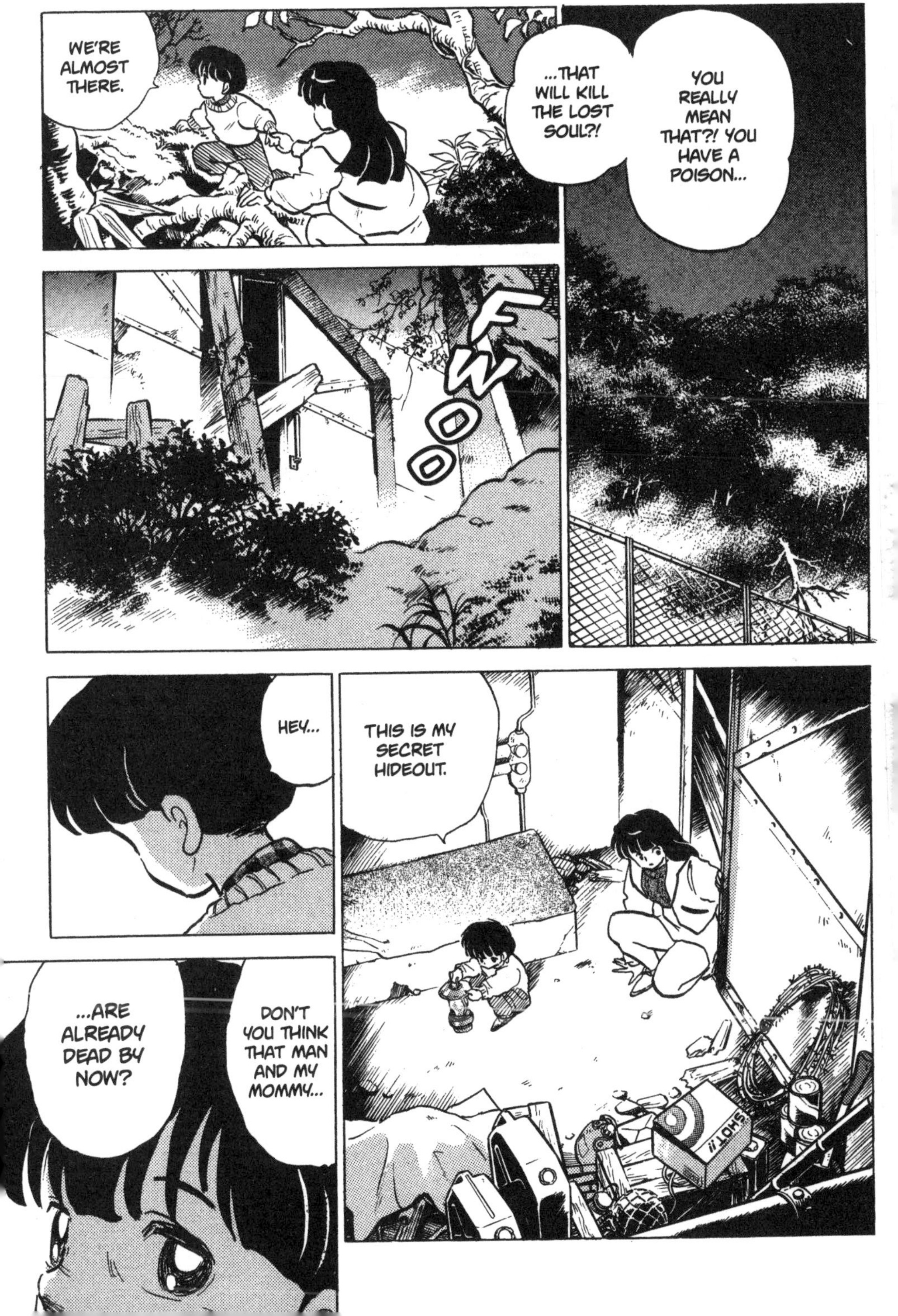
YOU REALLY MEAN THAT?! YOU HAVE A POISON...
...THAT WILL KILL THE LOST SOUL?!
WE'RE ALMOST THERE.
FWOO
THIS IS MY SECRET HIDEOUT.
HEY...
DON'T YOU THINK THAT MAN AND MY MOMMY...
...ARE ALREADY DEAD BY NOW?

"HE CAN'T LIVE ON HIS OWN."
SSHHH
"THERE MUST HAVE BEEN OTHERS BEFORE ME."
"OTHER WOMEN HE PICKED UP AND FED THE MERMAID FLESH TO..."
"HE'LL DO THE SAME THING AGAIN."
MANA...
MANA-AAA!!

YU... TA...
YUTA....
I HAVE TO GET RID OF THAT GUY.

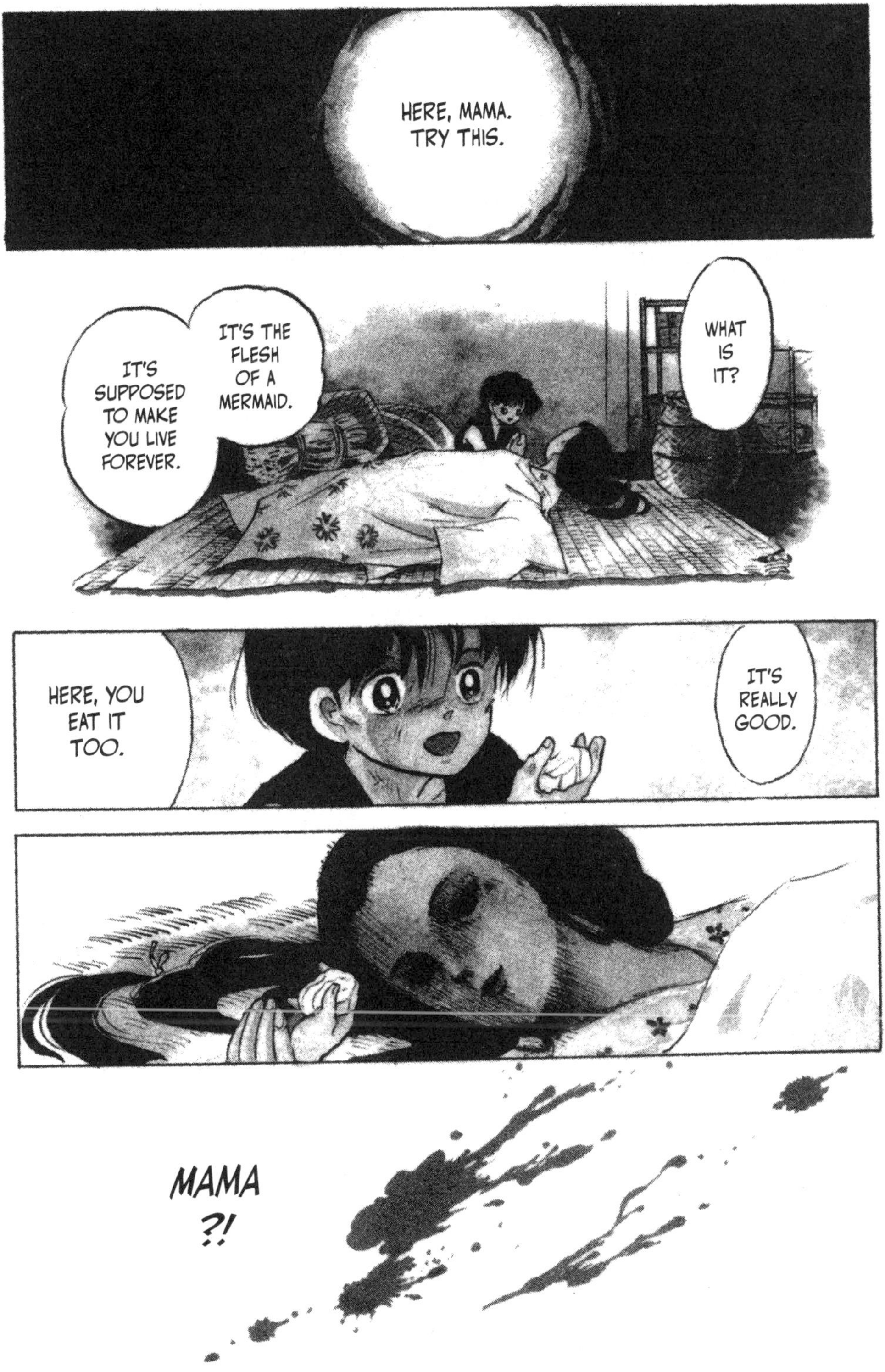
HERE, MAMA. TRY THIS.
WHAT IS IT?
IT'S THE FLESH OF A MERMAID.
IT'S SUPPOSED TO MAKE YOU LIVE FOREVER.
IT'S REALLY GOOD.
HERE, YOU EAT IT TOO.
MAMA ?!

Chapter II: Mermaid's Scar, Part 2

WAAHH!
FWOOO
...

YOU'RE COVERED WITH BLOOD.
...
YOU MUST HAVE REALLY SQUIRMED AROUND.
DOESN'T IT HURT?
CHOMP
WHOA!
YOU'RE A TOUGH ONE, AREN'T YOU?

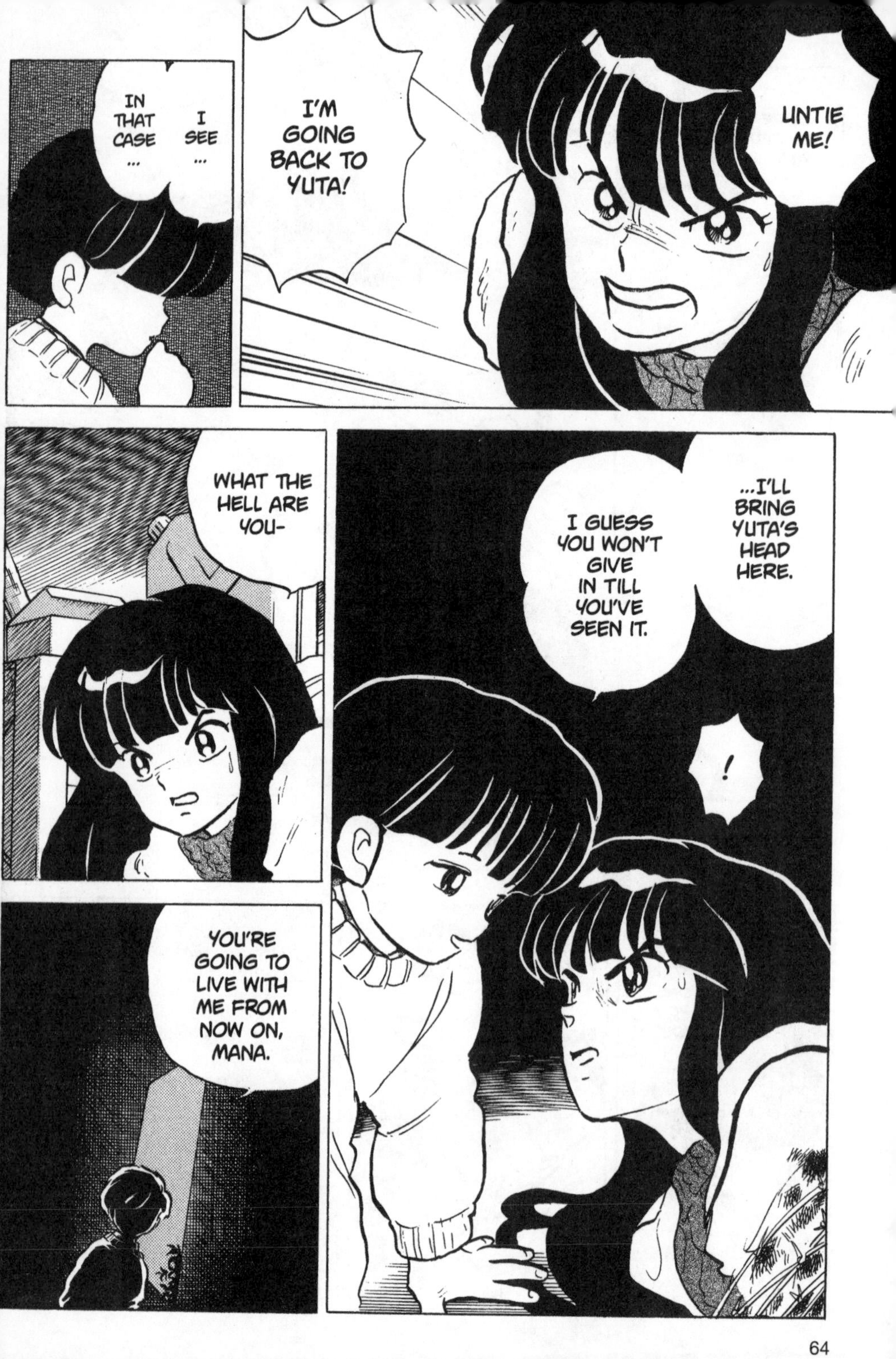
UNTIE ME!
I'M GOING BACK TO YUTA!
I SEE ...
IN THAT CASE ...
...I'LL BRING YUTA'S HEAD HERE.
I GUESS YOU WON'T GIVE IN TILL YOU'VE SEEN IT.
!
WHAT THE HELL ARE YOU-
YOU'RE GOING TO LIVE WITH ME FROM NOW ON, MANA.

HFF...
HFF...
HFF...
HFF...
SHA
MANA... WHERE ARE YOU?!
HWOO

HWOOO
TMP
SLW

FLUMP
HEY...
SO YOU STILL ...
...HAVEN'T COME BACK TO LIFE.
PLEASE.
YOU'VE GOT TO TELL ME WHERE THAT KID IS.
YOU'RE WASTING YOUR TIME.
SHE DOESN'T KNOW A THING.
!

THE MERMAID FLESH WASN'T COMPLETELY EFFECTIVE ON HER.
IT'S BEEN TAKING LONGER AND LONGER FOR HER TO COME BACK TO LIFE.
WELL, I'M DONE WITH HER ANYWAY.
I'LL CHOP HER HEAD OFF LATER.
WHA...
WHY, YOU-!
DASH
FLIPP

TMP
TMP
TMP
HOLD IT!
TMP
TMP
TMP
UNH!
WHAK
FIPP
FIPP
TAK
TAK
TAK
TMP
TMP
TMP
YOU LITTLE ...
WHAK
WHAK

AGH!
FWISH
?!
SHIK
PIANO WIRE ?!
HM.
I GUESS I SHOULDN'T HAVE EXPECTED YOUR HEAD TO COME OFF JUST LIKE THAT.
WHA-

GRP
BLAM
W...
WHY ARE YOU ...?
IT'S THE REAL THING.
I FILCHED THIS IN THE LAST WAR.
FLUMP

AS LONG AS YOU'RE ALIVE, MANA WILL KEEP TRYING TO RUN AWAY.
THE WAY THIS ONE DID.
I HAVE NO CHOICE.
HMPH.
I'VE HAD IT WITH YOU!
TMP
BLAM

NOBODY KNOWS BETTER THAN I DO...
...ABOUT HOW HARD IT IS TO BE ALONE.
ABOUT THE PAIN OF BEING IMMORTAL.
LET ME TELL YOU SOME-THING.
I'VE LIVED 500 YEARS ALL ALONE.
WHAM
GRP

SO I WON'T BUY YOUR EXCUSES!
JUST HOW MANY PEOPLE HAVE YOU FED MERMAID FLESH?!
FINE.
JUST KILL ME, THEN.
...
FSH

AH!!
!
SHUNK
LOOKS LIKE YOU HAVEN'T HAD IT ROUGH ENOUGH.
SUCKER.
FLUMP
UNHH...
Y... YOU LITTLE...

I'VE LIVED IN THIS FORM FOR 800 YEARS.
I DON'T HAVE TO SIT HERE AND BE LECTURED BY AN OVERSIZED YOUNG PUNK LIKE YOU.
!
E-EIGHT HUNDRED YEARS...?

NOW WHO WAS THE FIRST PERSON I EVER FED MERMAID FLESH TO?
WHAT IS IT?
IT'S THE FLESH OF A MERMAID.
IT'S SUPPOSED TO MAKE YOU LIVE FOREVER.
HERE, MAMA. TRY THIS.
IT'S REALLY GOOD.
HERE, YOU EAT IT TOO.

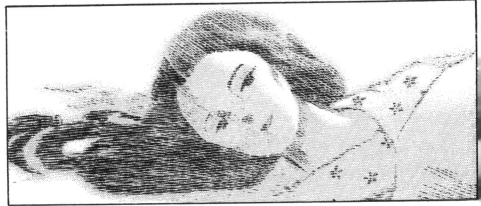

I GUESS ...
I GUESS THAT WAS MY REAL MAMA.
I CAN'T REMEMBER.

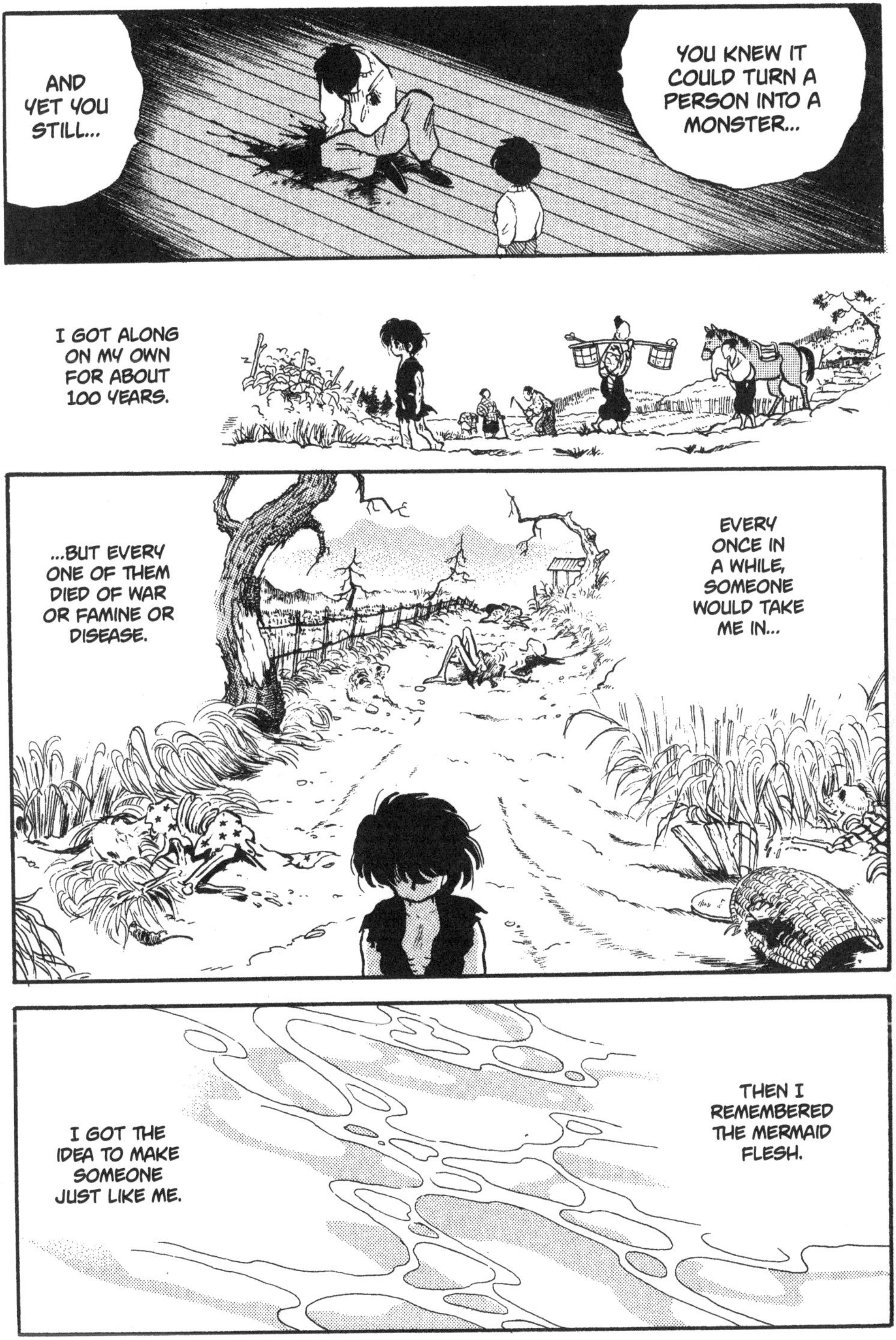
YOU KNEW IT COULD TURN A PERSON INTO A MONSTER...
AND YET YOU STILL...
I GOT ALONG ON MY OWN FOR ABOUT 100 YEARS.
EVERY ONCE IN A WHILE, SOMEONE WOULD TAKE ME IN...
...BUT EVERY ONE OF THEM DIED OF WAR OR FAMINE OR DISEASE.
THEN I REMEMBERED THE MERMAID FLESH.
I GOT THE IDEA TO MAKE SOMEONE JUST LIKE ME.

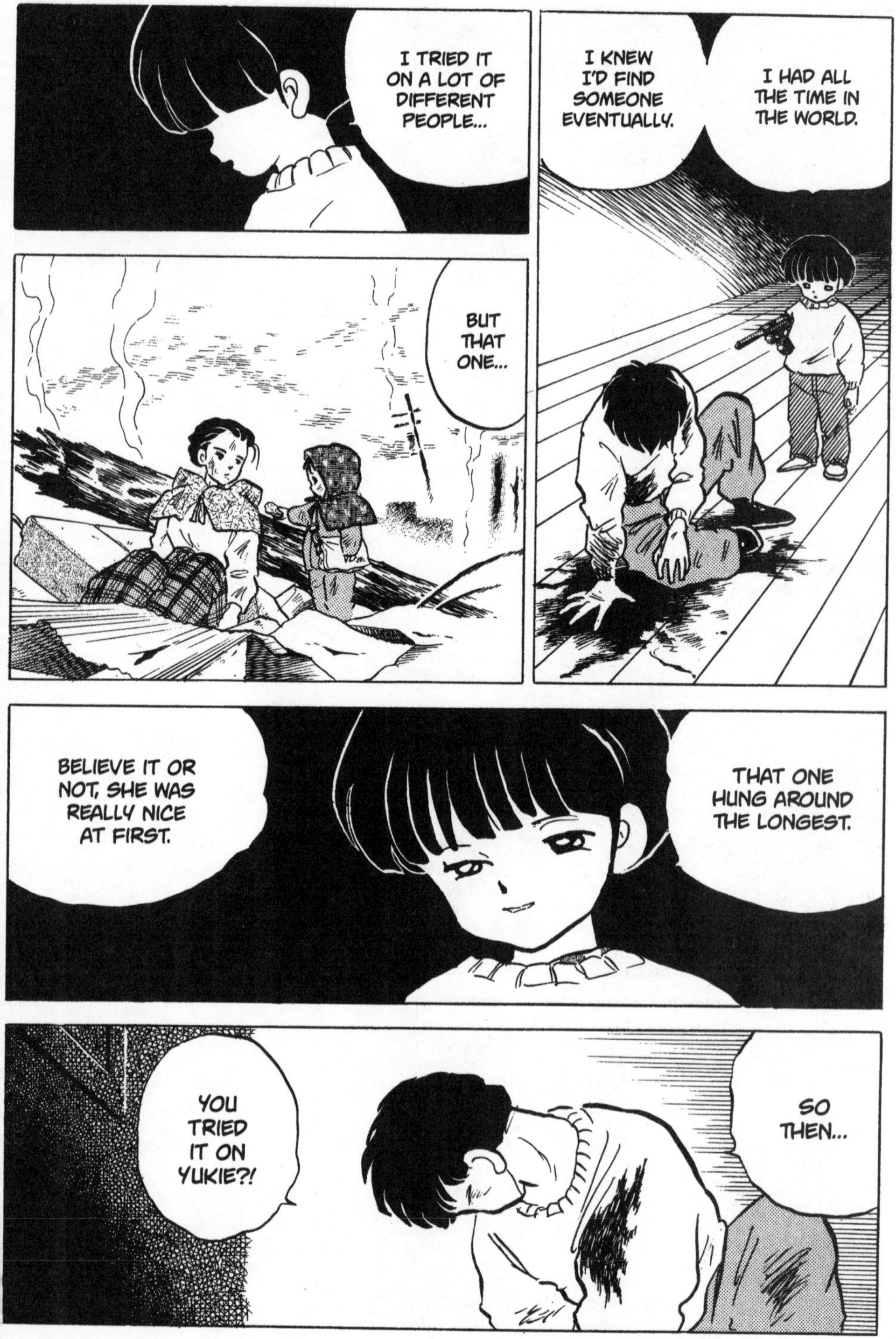
I HAD ALL THE TIME IN THE WORLD.
I KNEW I'D FIND SOMEONE EVENTUALLY.
I TRIED IT ON A LOT OF DIFFERENT PEOPLE...
BUT THAT ONE...
THAT ONE HUNG AROUND THE LONGEST.
BELIEVE IT OR NOT, SHE WAS REALLY NICE AT FIRST.
SO THEN...
YOU TRIED IT ON YUKIE?!

SHE...
SHE WAS SO KIND TO YOU.
DID YOU REALLY NOT GIVE A DAMN...
...WHETHER SHE DIED OR TURNED INTO A MONSTER?!
I'M SORRY.
I WISH I COULD HAVE STAYED WITH YOU LONGER.

PEOPLE LIKE YOU AND ME CAN'T LET OURSELVES LOVE OTHERS AS EASILY AS THAT.
IT WOULD BE TOO PAINFUL.

FWOOO
SKRSH
HFF... HFF...
HFF...
HFF... HFF...
SKSHH

SKRSHHH
SKIK
UNH!
FWUMP
VRN VRN VRN
HEY!!
GAH!!
JOLT

UNTIE ME!
AND BE QUICK ABOUT IT!
HUH?
ER...
THAT BRAT.
HE WON'T GET AWAY WITH THIS!
HWOO
TMP
SKSH
HOLD STILL.
FWISH

SWAY
FWISH
FAKK
FLUMP
UNH
...
WOBBLE
MAYBE I SHOULD SHOOT HIM AGAIN.

SKSH
MA...NA...
UNH...
ARE YOU AFRAID TO DIE?

TMP TMP TMP TMP
YUTA!!

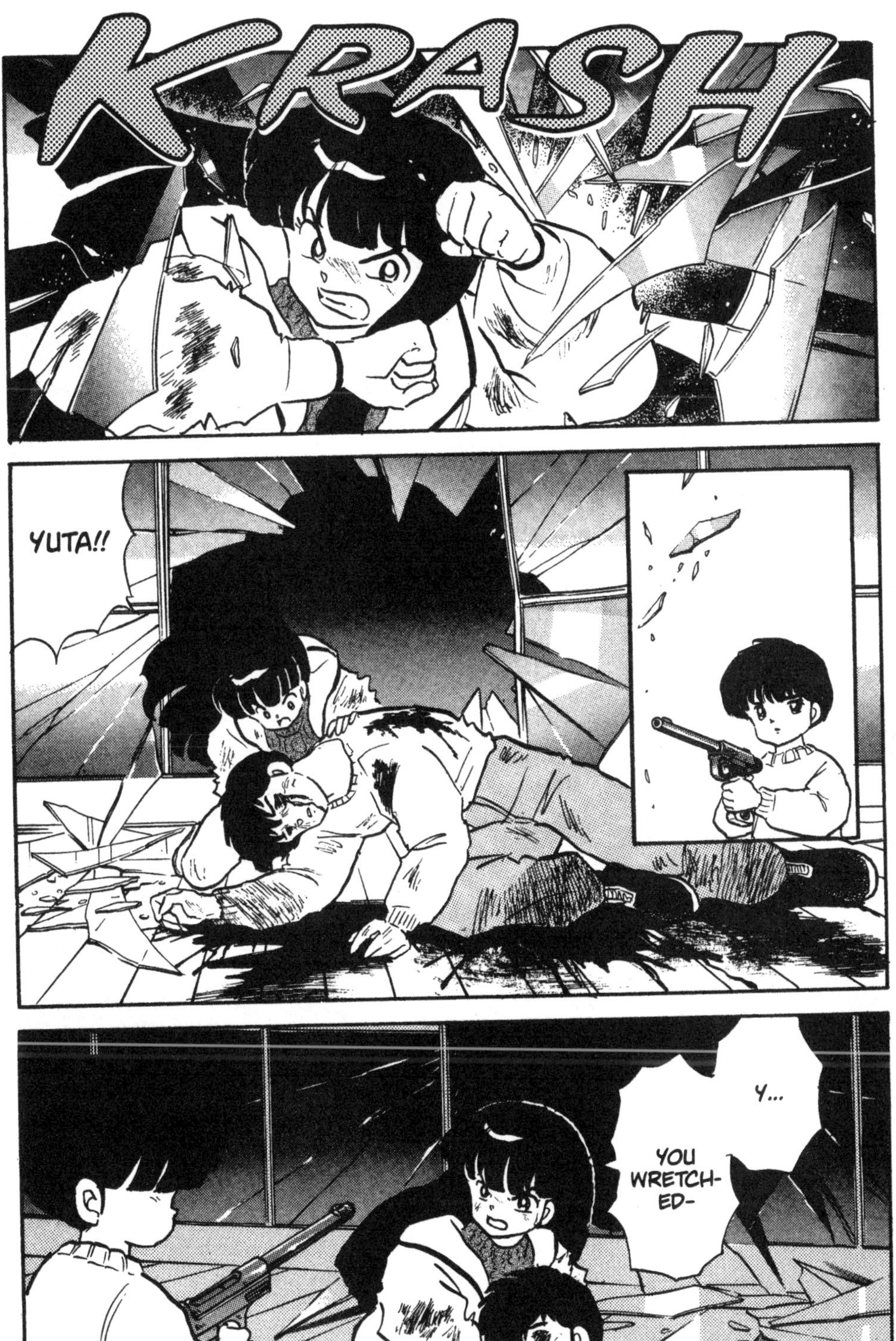
KRASH
YUTA!!
Y...
YOU WRETCH-ED-

BLAM
THAK
UNH!
DON'T GET IN THE WAY.
KLUNK
!

SHUNK

VWP
FWSH
SHUNK
TMP
TMP
THMP

JUST YOU TRY...
JUST YOU TRY AND KILL YUTA...
KRAK
I'LL KILL YOU!!
IF IT TAKES MY WHOLE LIFE, I'LL TRACK YOU DOWN...
...AND THEN I'LL TAKE THAT CURSED HEAD OF YOURS.

WITHOUT YUTA...
...IT WOULD BE THE ONLY THING LEFT FOR ME TO DO.
HMPH.

SWAY
FLUMP
WHAT A HORRIBLE GIRL.
I'VE NEVER MET SUCH A HORRIBLE GIRL.
HEY.
I'VE DECIDED TO LET YOU LIVE A WHILE LONGER.

HEY ...
WAKE UP.
SHF
SHE'S DEAD FOR REAL.

HMPH.
WIPE

GLUB
GLUB
GLUB
GLUB
KRAKL
KRAKL
!
BWOOSH
THE MERMAID FLESH.
THERE'S PLENTY LEFT.

SEE YOU.
IF YOU'RE STILL ALIVE, THAT IS.
TMP
KRAKL KRAKL KRAKL
HEY!
UNGH...
GRAB
FWOOSH
BWOOSH
FWOOM

VROOM
FWOO
KLANG KLANG KLANG
KLANG KLANG KLANG

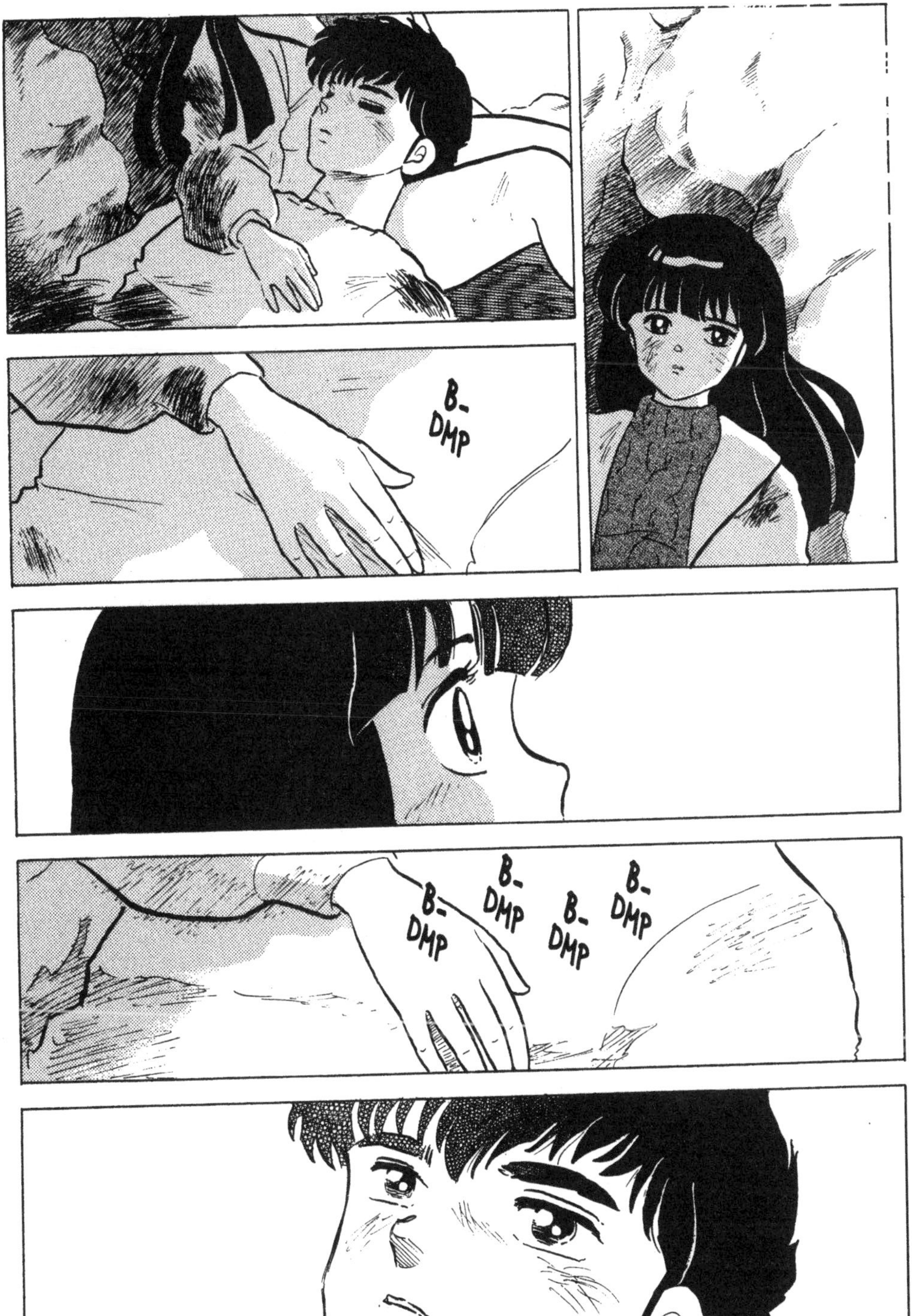
B-DMP
B-DMP
B-DMP
B-DMP
B-DMP

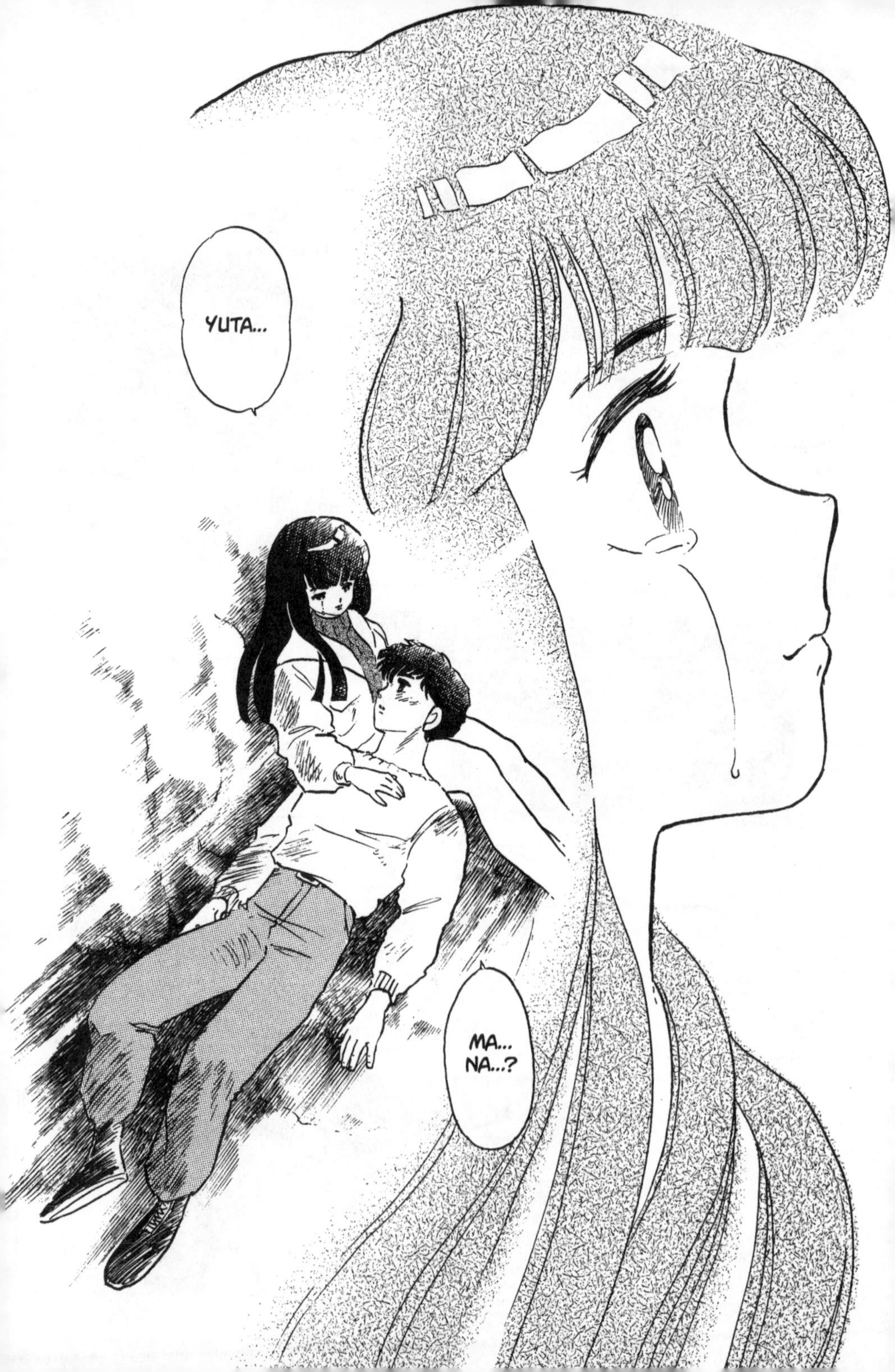
MA... NA...?
YUTA...

WHERE'S THE KID...?
HE ESCAPED WITH THE MERMAID FLESH.
LET'S GO AFTER HIM.
SKREE SK-SKREE
TURBO INTERCOOLER
HONNNK

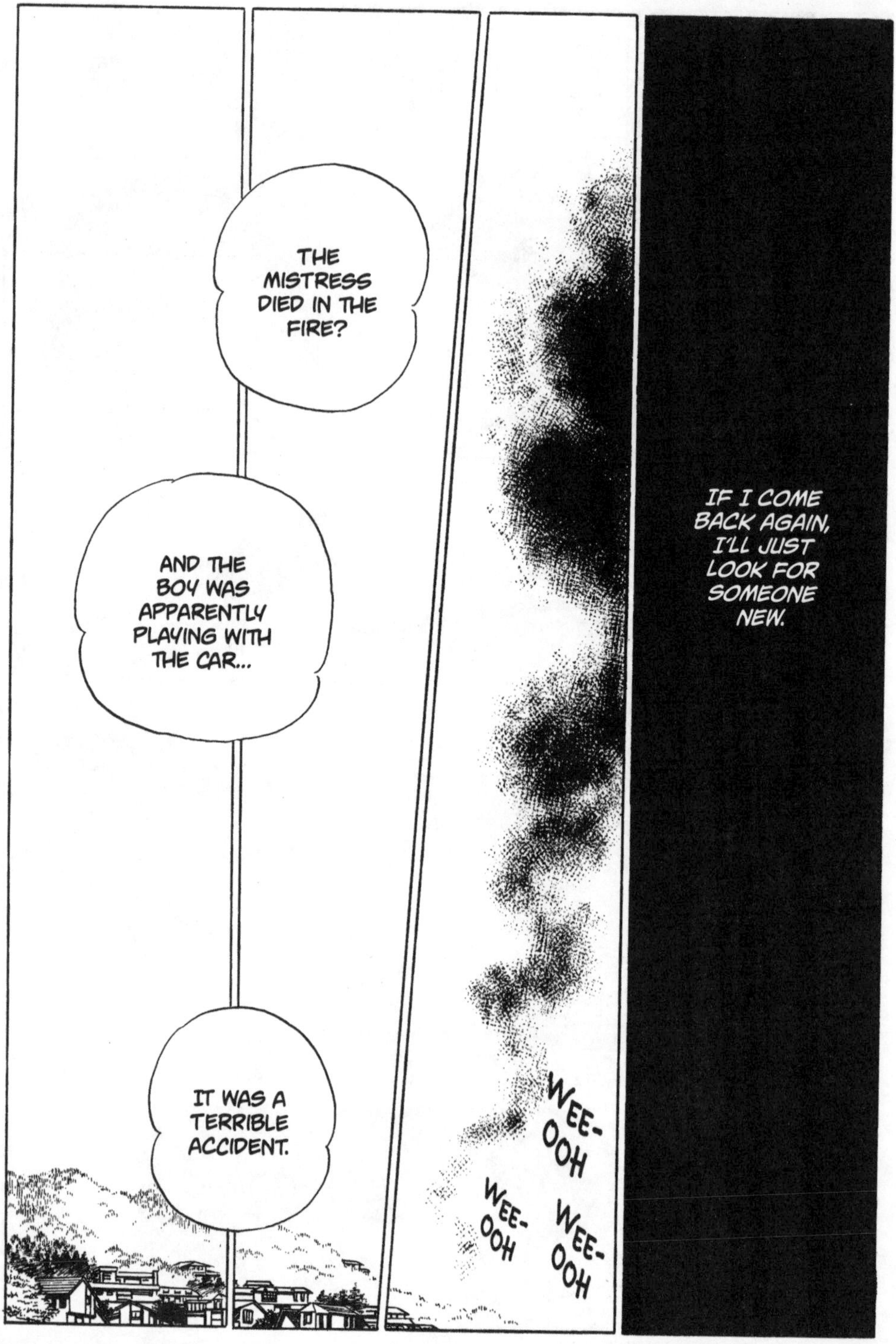
IF I COME BACK AGAIN, I'LL JUST LOOK FOR SOMEONE NEW.
WEE-OOH
WEE-OOH
WEE-OOH
THE MISTRESS DIED IN THE FIRE?
AND THE BOY WAS APPARENTLY PLAYING WITH THE CAR...
IT WAS A TERRIBLE ACCIDENT.

WHAT ABOUT YUKIE, THE HELPER?
THEY HAVEN'T FOUND HER.
SHE WAS PROBABLY SPENDING THE NIGHT ...
THE POOR THING...
AND SHE WAS SUCH A SWEET GIRL...
YUKIE...
I'M SORRY.

SAY, MANA...
HM?
YOU WERE CRYING WHEN I CAME BACK TO LIFE, WEREN'T YOU?
UH-HUH.
WERE YOU AFRAID?
DON'T BE STUPID!
WELL, IT'S JUST THAT I...
I'VE NEVER SEEN YOU CRY BEFORE.
YEAH.
THAT WAS THE FIRST TIME I'VE EVER CRIED.

I THOUGHT TO MYSELF, "YUTA IS ALIVE."
I WAS SO HAPPY, AND THEN TEARS JUST STARTED COMING OUT.

Mermaid's Scar / The End

MERMAID SAGA

THEY SAY TOKUGAWA'S TAKEN POWER.
IS THAT SO? WHAT'S BECOME OF TOYOTOMI? *
WHAT'S WRONG, TAKÉ?
YOU'RE NOT FEELING WELL AGAIN?
SWAY
FLUMP
TAKÉ...!!
WHAT IS IT?!
AGH!!
THE BOY'S TURNED TO BONES!!
FSSS
TAKÉ!!
MMBL
MMBL
...
THIS IS HIS DOING.

* The Tokugawa clan wrested control of Japan from the Toyotomi clan in the first years of the 17th century.

Chapter 12: The Ash Princess

NOW, LADIES AND GENTLE- MEN.
I TRUST YOU'VE ALL HEARD OF THE MERMAID?
THE FIGURE OF A CELESTIAL MAIDEN, THE VOICE OF A SKYLARK...
AND THOSE WHO EAT THEIR FLESH GAIN ETERNAL YOUTH AND LONGEVITY.
MRMR
MRMR
MRMR

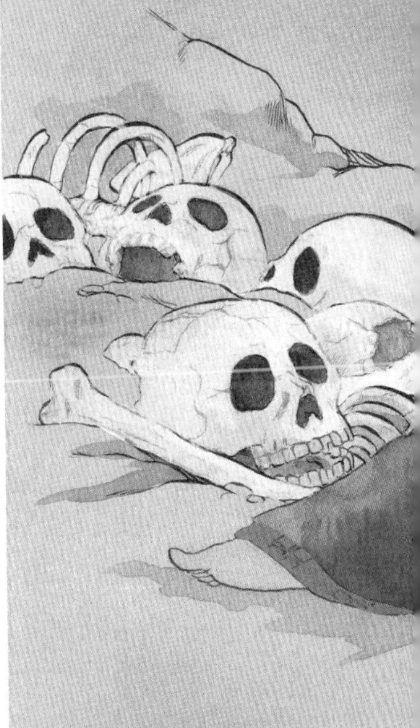

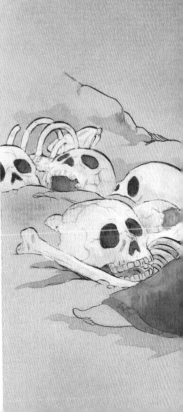

TAKE A GOOD, LONG LOOK AT THE MERMAID I HAVE HERE.
JUST LOOKING WILL MAKE YOU LIVE LONGER.
SPLSH
SPLSH
OOH
IT'S REAL ...
IT'S THE REAL THING!
SPLISH
TMP
THIS GIRL ATE THE FLESH OF A MERMAID AT THE AGE OF 12, GAINING ETERNAL YOUTH AND LONGEVITY.

SLICE
EEE!
HO HO HO. NO NEED TO WORRY.
WIPE WIPE
SEE? GOOD AS NEW.
IT'S HEALED!
MRMR
MRMR
HOW CAN IT BE?
THIS IS THE EFFECT OF THE MERMAID FLESH.
EAT THIS MARVELOUS MERMAID FLESH, AND YOU TOO CAN HAVE ETERNAL LIFE AND GOOD HEALTH.

...
I'LL BUY IT!
GIVE ME SOME OF THAT MERMAID FLESH.
THANK YOU, THANK YOU.
I'M CERTAIN ...
...THAT GIRL...
YOU SAY YOU BOUGHT THE FLESH OF A MERMAID?!
YEAH. AT ONE OF THE SIDE-SHOWS AT THE MARKET.
D-DID YOU EAT IT?!
YEAH.
IT TASTED KINDA LIKE CARP.

LOOK AT THIS.
I SLIPPED ON A MOUNTAIN PATH...
...BUT EVEN THIS LITTLE SCRATCH WON'T HEAL...
I WONDER IF THAT WAS JUST CARP.
HEH
I'M GLAD TO HEAR THAT.
TAKE CARE.
CARP MEAT...
IF THAT'S THE CASE...
...THEN I GUESS THE MERMAID HE MENTIONED...
...WAS JUST A FRAUD TOO.
"IF YOU WANT TO RETURN TO NORMAL..."
"...FIND A MERMAID."
KAW KAW

NATSUME.
NATSUME.
NOW WHERE IS THAT GIRL?
MAYBE SHE WENT OFF TO LOOK FOR SOMETHING TO FEED THE MERMAID.
SPLSH
MNCH
MNCH
MNCH
HMM.
I'LL SAVE THE REST FOR THE MERMAID.
TWITCH
TWITCH
EVIL SPIRIT!

TMP
SHNG
TO NIRVANA WITH YOU!!
HM?

I'M HUNGRY.
EEK!
TMP TMP
TMP TMP
FWAK
AHHH!!
!

DMP
AH!
VSH
STOP!!
DASH
WHAM
SKSH
SHK
VSH

IF YOU DON'T HOLD STILL, YOU'RE GOING TO BLEED TO DEATH!
HEY.
FWP
AH...
THUNK
THUNK
TAKE THAT!
GRR!
THUNK
THUNK
WAHHH
BUT HE-!!
SNFF
SNFF
...

NATSUME.
NATSUME.
PA!
YOUR PA'S PRETTY OLD, ISN'T HE?
...
DON'T TELL ANYONE...
...BUT I DON'T THINK HE'S MY REAL PA.
YOU POOR THING.
LET YOUR PA HAVE A LOOK.

YOU SAY A MONK ATTACKED YOU?
HE SAID, "TO NIRVANA WITH YOU!"
SPLSH
I WONDER WHAT THAT MEANS.
...
I WONDER.
ARE YOU THE ONE SELLING MERMAID FLESH, OLD MAN?
I HEARD ABOUT YOU.
THAT'S RIGHT.
YUTA, WAS IT?
BY WAY OF THANKING YOU, I'LL GIVE YOU A PIECE FOR FREE.
NO THANKS.
THAT'S A SLEAZY WAY TO MAKE A LIVING.

HO HO HO.
NOT AT ALL.
WHAT I'M DOING IS SELLING THE DREAM OF ETERNAL YOUTH AND LONGEVITY.
LIVING LONG ISN'T EVERYTHING, YOU KNOW.
YOU THINK SO?
THERE YOU ARE, NATSUME. ALL BETTER.
CAN YOU MOVE IT?
YAY! GOOD AS NEW.
WHAT ...?!

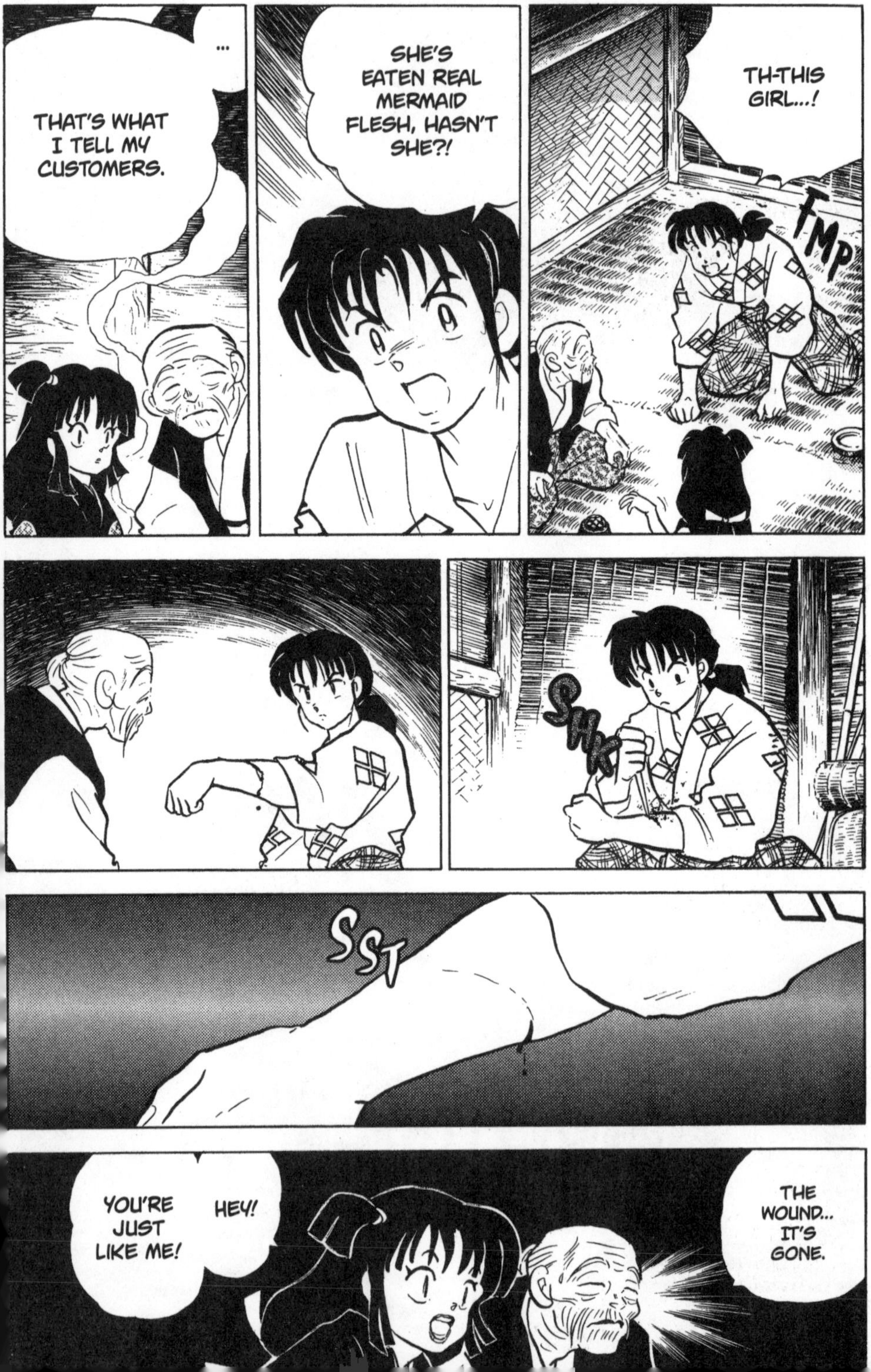
TH-THIS GIRL...!
FMP
SHE'S EATEN REAL MERMAID FLESH, HASN'T SHE?!
...
THAT'S WHAT I TELL MY CUSTOMERS.
SHK
SST
THE WOUND... IT'S GONE.
HEY!
YOU'RE JUST LIKE ME!

I ATE THE FLESH OF A MERMAID.
I'VE BEEN ALIVE SOME 210 YEARS.
AS YOU SEE, EVEN IF I HURT MYSELF, THE WOUND HEALS IN NO TIME.
I'VE DIED A DOZEN TIMES, BUT EVERY TIME I COME BACK TO LIFE.
I WANT TO RETURN TO NORMAL.
I WAS TOLD THE ONLY WAY IS TO FIND A MERMAID.
THAT'S ALL?
WE'VE GOT A MERMAID RIGHT HERE.
SPLSH
...!
SPLSH

KEEEE
SPLASH
SPLASH
W—
WHAT IS THIS?!
JUST A SIDESHOW ATTRACTION.
NOT THE MERMAID YOU'RE LOOKING FOR, I GATHER.
KEE!
BUT... BUT YOU...
UNFORTU-NATELY...

...THIS GIRL HAS NOT EATEN THE FLESH OF A MERMAID.
IT'S GETTING LATE.
WE CAN TALK TOMORROW.
THIS PLACE ISN'T MUCH, BUT IT KEEPS THE RAIN OFF.
YOU'RE WELCOME TO SPEND THE NIGHT.
WHAT'S GOING ON HERE?
THIS GIRL NATSUME...
IF SHE HASN'T EATEN MERMAID FLESH, THEN HOW...?
FMP

AAHH!
CHOMP
GRND GRND
WHAT ARE YOU DOING?!
VSH
N-NATSUME!
...
I'M SORRY. PLEASE...
PLEASE LEAVE!
OW...
THAT GIRL CAN REALLY BITE.
TMP

YOU...
YOU ALMOST HAD YOUR LIVER EATEN, DIDN'T YOU?
YOU'RE THAT MONK...
WHAT DO YOU MEAN ABOUT MY LIVER?
THAT OLD MAN AND GIRL...
WHO ARE THEY?
AND THAT THING THAT LOOKS LIKE A CROSS BETWEEN A MONKEY AND A FISH...
THIS IS ALL SO CONFUSING.
THAT GIRL... IS NOT OF THIS WORLD.

YEARS AGO I GATHERED TOGETHER HER BONES ...
...AND MADE HER.
BONES ?!
I USED ...
...A TECHNIQUE KNOWN AS HAN GON.
KRAKL KRAKL
DECADES AGO, THE COUNTRY WAS TORN BY CONSTANT WARS.
I WOULD WALK FROM VILLAGE TO VILLAGE...
...ADMINIS-TERING LAST RITES.
IT WAS THEN ...
...THAT I MET THAT MAN.

IN HIS ARMS HE HELD A SMALL SKULL.
THE SIGHT OF IT WAS TOO HEART-BREAKING TO BEAR.
I INVITED THE MAN TO MY TEMPLE.
THIS IS THE *HAN GON* TECHNIQUE. I HAVE VERY LITTLE EXPERIENCE, SO I CAN'T GUARANTEE THAT IT WILL WORK.
BUT IF I USE THIS MERMAID LIVER...
...THAT HAS BEEN IN THIS TEMPLE FOR CENTURIES...
A MERMAID LIVER...

I PAINTED THE BONES WITH ARSENIC ...
...RUBBED TOGETHER STRAW-BERRY AND CHICKWEED LEAVES...
...BOILED ALOES-WOOD AND MILK...
THE BONES TOOK ON THE FORM OF A GIRL AND CAME TO LIFE.
YOU CAN'T IMAGINE THE MAN'S JOY.
IT WAS AS IF HE HAD BEEN BROUGHT BACK TO LIFE ALONG WITH THE GIRL.
HOW-EVER...
...THE GIRL WOULD CATCH DOGS AND CATS...
EVEN ATTACK THOSE WHO HAD FALLEN IN BATTLE...
SHE'D EAT THEIR LIVERS WHILE THEY WERE STILL ALIVE...
...JUST AS YOU AND I WOULD EAT RICE.
BY THE TIME I DETERMINED THAT I MUST RETURN THE GIRL TO BONES AGAIN...
...THE MAN HAD ALREADY DISAPPEARED WITH THE GIRL.

AND THE OLD MAN WHO RUNS THE SIDE-SHOW IS THAT MAN?
THE MERMAID HE EXHIBITS...
MY GUESS IS HE MEMORIZED THE *HAN GON* TECHNIQUE BY WATCHING ME AND MADE THAT THING FROM THE BONES OF A MONKEY AND A FISH.
TOYING WITH LIFE IN THAT WAY...
...IS THE LEAST OF IT.
WHILE TRAVELING IN SEARCH OF HIM...
...AGAIN AND AGAIN ...
...I CAME ACROSS STORIES OF PEOPLE WHO HAD BEEN BROUGHT BACK TO LIFE, ONLY TO RETURN SUDDENLY TO BONES.
YOU'RE SAYING THE OLD MAN HAS BEEN TRAVELING AROUND PERFORMING A HALF-BAKED VERSION OF THE *HAN GON* TECHNIQUE?
THE REASON NATSUME HASN'T RETURNED TO BONES AFTER ALL THESE DECADES...

...IS THAT I USED THE LIVER OF A MERMAID TO REVIVE HER.
AT THE AGE OF 12, THIS GIRL ATE THE FLESH OF A MERMAID...
SHE SURE DOESN'T LOOK LIKE AN EVIL SPIRIT.
AH!
YUTA!
TMP TMP

SORRY ABOUT LAST NIGHT.
DID IT HURT?
GRIN
YOU ...
YOU MEANT TO EAT MY LIVER?
YEP!
AFTER ALL, YOU'VE GOT AN IMMORTAL LIVER.
I WONDERED WHAT IT WOULD TASTE LIKE.
NATSU-ME.
OOPS. I ALMOST FORGOT ABOUT THE SHOW.
SEE YOU LATER!
"THAT GIRL IS NOT OF THIS WORLD."
"SHE MUST BE RETURNED TO BONES."

I AM GOING TO FAST AND CLEANSE MY BODY IN ORDER TO STRENGTHEN MY DHARMA.
FOR SEVEN DAYS I'LL BE UNABLE TO MOVE.
THAT'S WHY I'M GOING TO ASK THIS FAVOR OF YOU.
YOU WANT ME TO BE YOUR ACCOMPLICE? HELP TURN NATSUME BACK INTO...
ALL YOU HAVE TO DO IS KEEP AN EYE ON THEM.
"THAT GIRL WILL BE MUCH HAPPIER IN NIRVANA..."
"...THAN SHE IS DEVOURING THE LIVERS OF LIVING CREATURES AND CARRYING ON THIS WRETCHED EXISTENCE."
SIMPLE AS THAT, HUH?

YUTA!
DON'T YOU HAVE TO HELP WITH THE SIDESHOW?
PA'S GOT OTHER WORK TO DO.
IS IT TRUE YOU NEVER GET ANY OLDER, YUTA?
YOU'LL NEVER BE A GROWN-UP?
WATCH YOUR TONGUE, KID. I AM A GROWN-UP.
HMM.
WHAT ABOUT YOUR MA AND PA?
THEY WENT ON TO THE NEXT WORLD A LONG, LONG TIME AGO.
THEN YOU'RE ALL ALONE.
I GUESS SO.

POOR THING.
WANT ME TO STAY WITH YOU?
...
NOT VERY LOYAL, ARE YOU?
WHAT'LL YOUR PA DO WITHOUT YOU?
I WONDER IF HE'S REALLY MY PA.
IT'S SO WEIRD.
I DON'T REMEM-BER ANYTHING ABOUT PA...
...OR ANYTHING ELSE THAT HAPPENED BEFORE I WOKE UP.
NATSUME!
YOU'VE COME BACK! YOU'VE COME BACK TO ME!
PA KEEPS GETTING OLDER AND OLDER...
...AND I JUST STAY LIKE THIS.

WE'VE SET THE PRINCESS'S BODY OUT IN THE GARDEN AND LET IT TURN TO BONES, JUST AS YOU SAID TO.
IS THIS GOOD ENOUGH?
YES, YOUR LORDSHIP. YOU HAVE MY WORD THAT I WILL BRING THE PRINCESS BACK TO LIFE.
BUT HOW...?
I'VE MASTERED THE *HAN GON* TECHNIQUE, YOU SEE.
HAN GON?
AH, I'VE HEARD OF IT BEFORE.

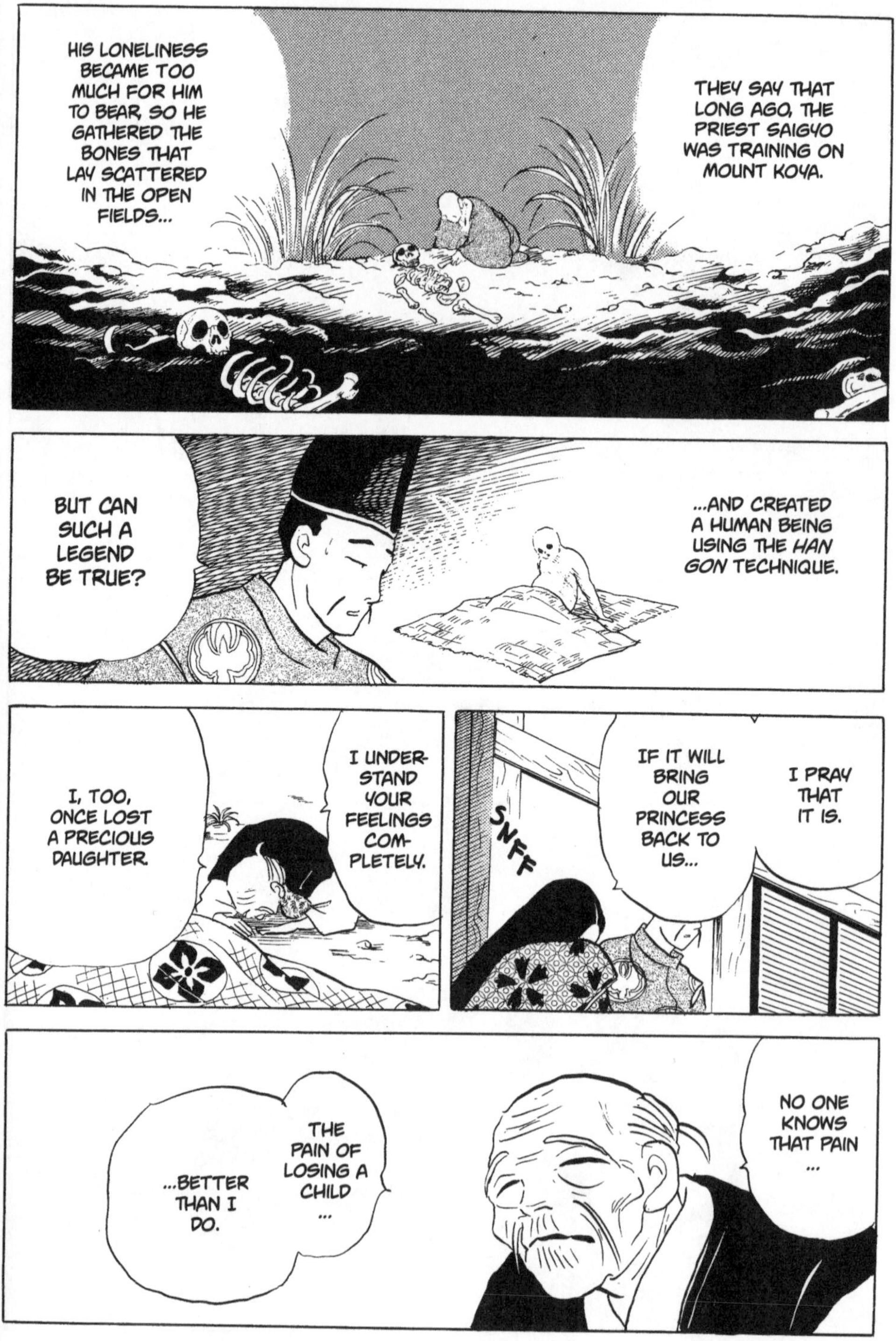
THEY SAY THAT LONG AGO, THE PRIEST SAIGYO WAS TRAINING ON MOUNT KOYA.
HIS LONELINESS BECAME TOO MUCH FOR HIM TO BEAR, SO HE GATHERED THE BONES THAT LAY SCATTERED IN THE OPEN FIELDS...
...AND CREATED A HUMAN BEING USING THE *HAN GON* TECHNIQUE.
BUT CAN SUCH A LEGEND BE TRUE?
I PRAY THAT IT IS.
IF IT WILL BRING OUR PRINCESS BACK TO US...
SNFF
I UNDER-STAND YOUR FEELINGS COM-PLETELY.
I, TOO, ONCE LOST A PRECIOUS DAUGHTER.
NO ONE KNOWS THAT PAIN ...
THE PAIN OF LOSING A CHILD ...
...BETTER THAN I DO.

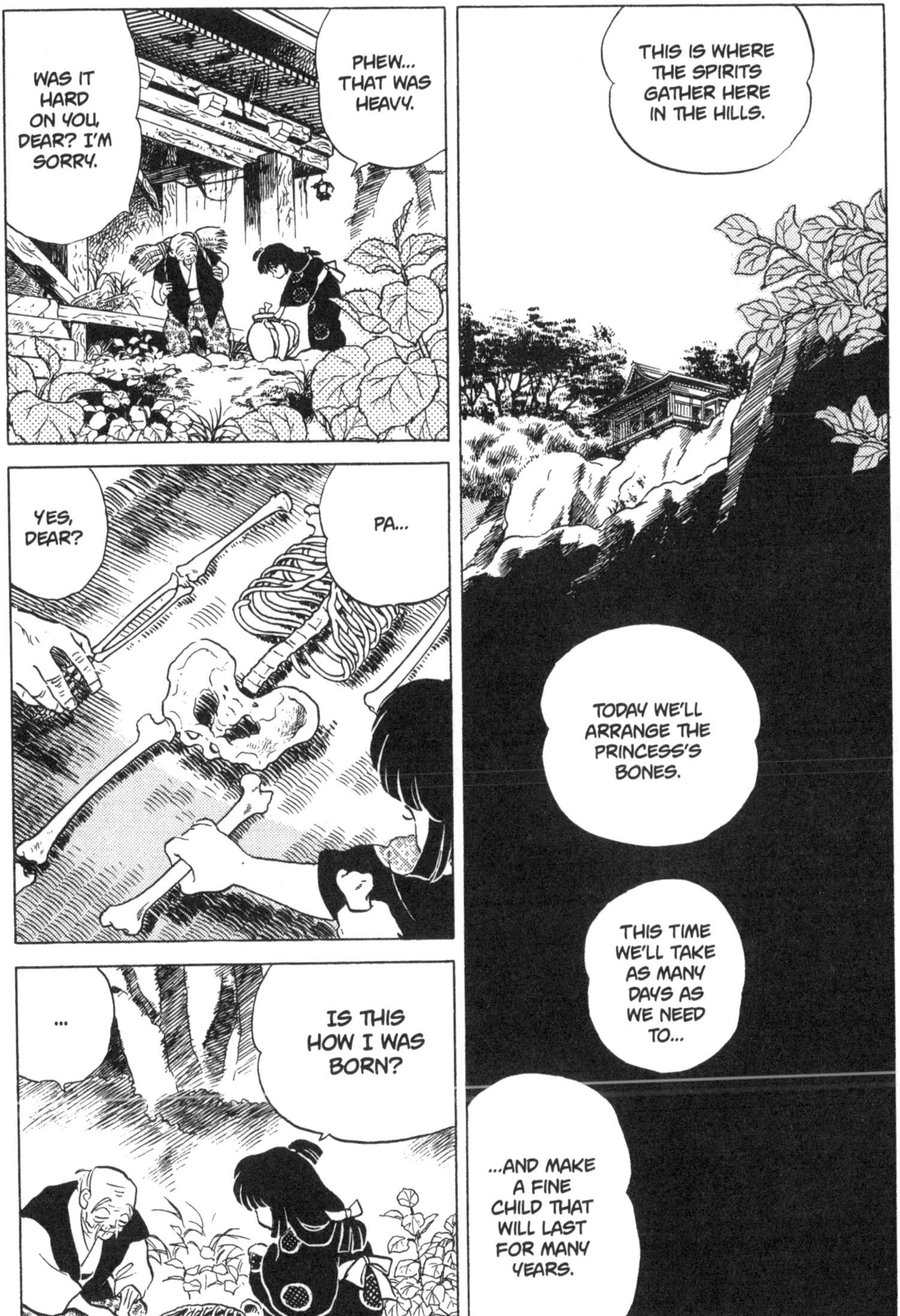
THIS IS WHERE THE SPIRITS GATHER HERE IN THE HILLS.
TODAY WE'LL ARRANGE THE PRINCESS'S BONES.
THIS TIME WE'LL TAKE AS MANY DAYS AS WE NEED TO...
...AND MAKE A FINE CHILD THAT WILL LAST FOR MANY YEARS.
PHEW... THAT WAS HEAVY.
WAS IT HARD ON YOU, DEAR? I'M SORRY.
PA...
YES, DEAR?
IS THIS HOW I WAS BORN?
...

WHY DO YOU DO THIS?
NATSUME, DON'T YOU REMEMBER?
THOSE WERE VIOLENT TIMES. NOTHING LIKE TODAY.
MANY, MANY PEOPLE DIED.
SO MANY PEOPLE DIED...
...THAT THE LIVING NO LONGER CRIED WHEN ANOTHER DIED.
NATSUME!
NATSUME ...!!
YOUR PA IS MAKING LIFE.
WHAT YOUR PA IS DOING IS GOOD.

"IT DOESN'T MATTER WHAT FORM IT TAKES..."
RSTL
MYAAAA!
MYAH
MNCH MNCH
"BEING ALIVE IS THE MOST IMPORTANT THING THERE IS."
WOOSH
SHHH
MERMAID!
I BROUGHT YOU SOME LIVER.
MERMAID ...?
PATTER PATTER PATTER

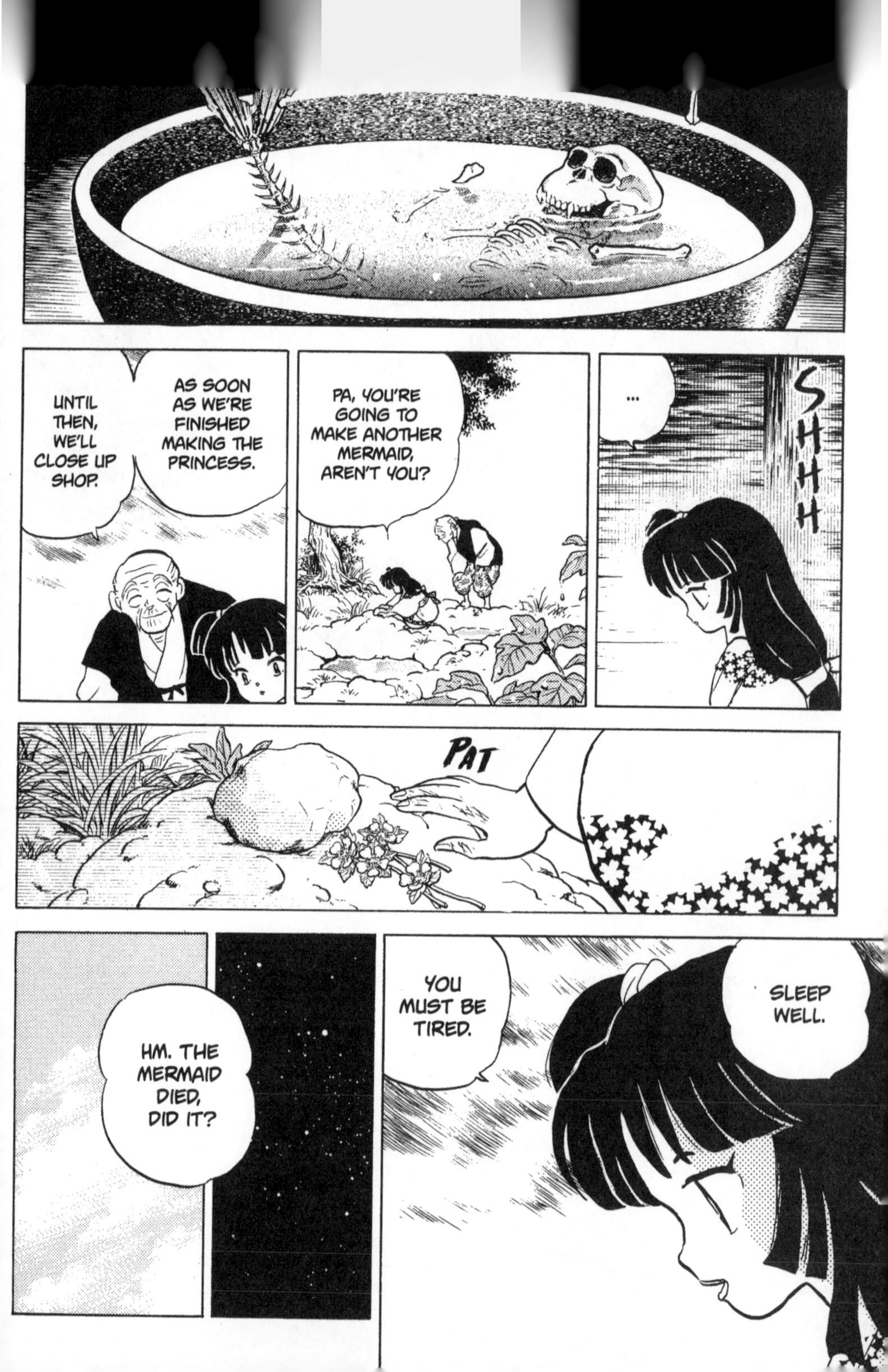
...
SHHH
PA, YOU'RE GOING TO MAKE ANOTHER MERMAID, AREN'T YOU?
AS SOON AS WE'RE FINISHED MAKING THE PRINCESS.
UNTIL THEN, WE'LL CLOSE UP SHOP.
PAT
SLEEP WELL.
YOU MUST BE TIRED.
HM. THE MERMAID DIED, DID IT?

WELL, DON'T LET IT GET YOU DOWN.
I'M NOT DOWN.
WHAT'RE YOU DOING?
I'VE GOT TO EARN A LIVING EVERY ONCE IN A WHILE TOO.
HERE, HAVE A FISH LIVER.
SLURP
SIGH...
I FEEL SO HELP-LESS.
AT LEAST IF I COULD BECOME A GROWN-UP...
...I COULD GET BY ON MY OWN...
...AFTER PA PASSES AWAY.
OH YEAH?
HMPH.

"THAT GIRL WILL BE MUCH HAPPIER IN NIRVANA..."
"...THAN SHE IS DEVOURING THE LIVERS OF LIVING CREATURES AND CARRYING ON THIS WRETCHED EXISTENCE."
BUT SHE'S ALIVE.
AND SHE'S THINKING ABOUT HOW TO GO ON LIVING.
NATSUME... HOW WOULD YOU LIKE TO GET AWAY FROM HERE?
WOULD YOU LIKE...
...TO COME WITH ME?

GASP
WHEN?
THE SOONER THE BETTER.
"FOR SEVEN DAYS I WILL STRENGTHEN MY DHARMA...AND THEN I'LL RETURN NATSUME TO BONES."
TODAY'S THE SEVENTH DAY.
I'VE GOT TO GET YOU AWAY FROM HERE.
WAIT FOR ME.
I'LL GO GET MY PA.
I'D LIKE YOU TO SAY GOODBYE TO HIM TOO.
NATSUME ...

TMP
YUTA.
NATSUME TOLD ME EVERYTHING.
SHE'S WAITING HERE IN THE HILLS?
THAT'S RIGHT.
SHK
RSTL

NATSUME ...
THWAK
FWUMP
W... WHY...
DON'T TAKE NATSUME AWAY FROM ME.
NATSUME'S MY ONLY DAUGHTER.
I WON'T HAND HER OVER TO ANYONE.

HMM.
I WONDER WHERE PA IS.
WHAT SHOULD I DO?
IT WOULDN'T BE RIGHT TO JUST LEAVE WITHOUT SAYING ANYTHING.
AH!
HE MUST BE IN THE HILLS MAKING THE PRINCESS.
SHK SHK
SHK

FWOO
NATSUME.
YOUR WANDERING IS OVER. NIRVANA AWAITS.
HWOO

HWOOO
!
W... WHAT DO YOU THINK YOU'RE...
COME TO, HAVE YOU?
LYING HERE IS A POOR PRINCESS WHO DIED AT A TENDER AGE.

WHAT DO YOU INTEND TO DO ...
...WITH ME?
I'VE DECIDED ...
...TO TAKE YOUR IMMORTAL LIVER.
NATSUME IS STILL ALIVE TODAY...
...BECAUSE I USED THE LIVER OF A MERMAID.
SO YOUR LIVER MAY BE EFFECTIVE TOO.
ARE YOU...?

I-NYO-JU-JUTSU-YAKU-RYOKU-NO-ZO-SHO-ZO-SHU-SHU-SHOKU-ZO...
SHK SHK
IF I CAN JUST RETRIEVE...
...THE MERMAID'S LIVER THAT I USED...
...IN THE HAN GON PROCEDURE...
...YOU WILL BE FINISHED!!
VSH

VWSH
VWSH
"NATSUME... HOW WOULD YOU LIKE TO GET AWAY FROM HERE?"
"WOULD YOU LIKE TO COME WITH ME?"
YES!
I'LL GO WITH YOU, YUTA.
NGH
CHING
SHIK

SHUNK
AGHH!
THUNK
TAKE THAT!
DASH
YOU STUPID OLD MONK!
HFF HFF...
HFF HFF...
SWAY

FWOO
WUMP
STAY STILL.
HFF HFF
YOU'VE LIVED QUITE A LONG LIFE, HAVEN'T YOU?
THERE'S NO ONE LEFT TO CRY FOR YOU IF YOU DIE, IS THERE?
YOU MUSTN'T ...
...MAKE ANY MORE CHILDREN LIKE NATSUME.

WHAT DO YOU KNOW OF THE FEELINGS OF A MAN...
...WHO'S HAD HIS CHILD TAKEN AWAY FROM HIM?!
SHUNK
PA...

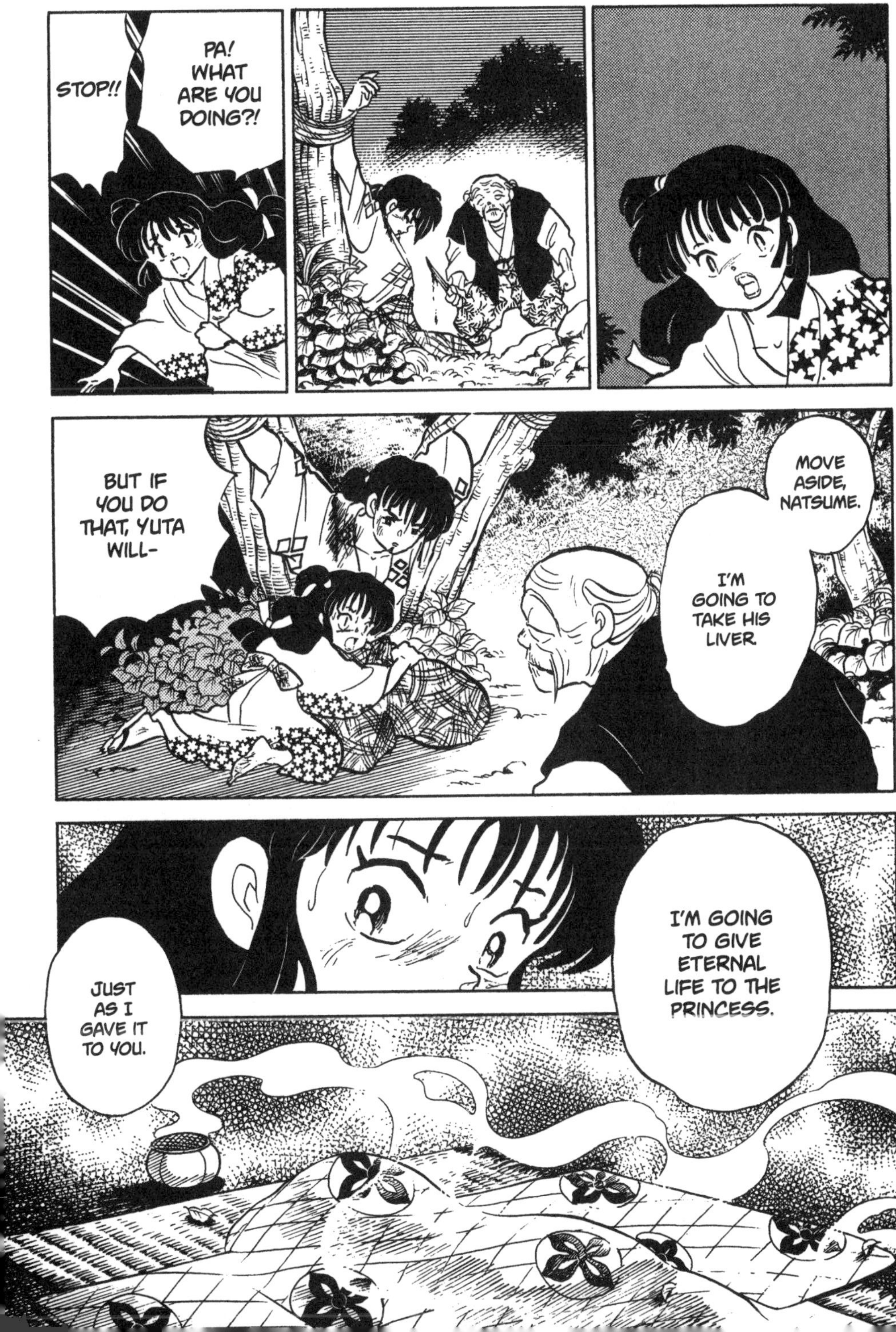
PA! WHAT ARE YOU DOING?!
STOP!!
MOVE ASIDE, NATSUME.
I'M GOING TO TAKE HIS LIVER.
BUT IF YOU DO THAT, YUTA WILL-
I'M GOING TO GIVE ETERNAL LIFE TO THE PRINCESS.
JUST AS I GAVE IT TO YOU.

FWMP
STOP!
STOP IT, PA!
SHHP
AH, SHE'S BEGUN TO FIRM UP.

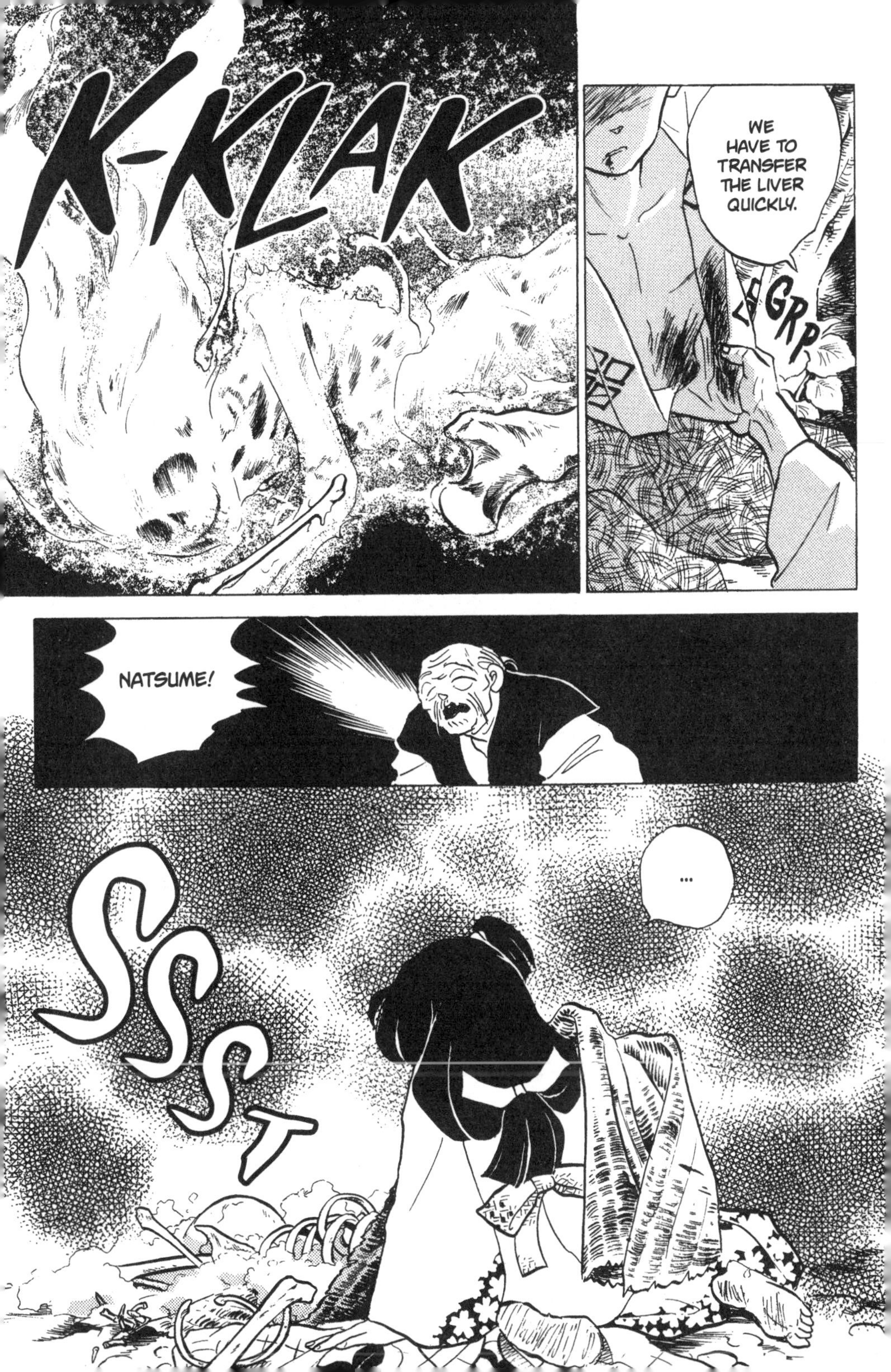
WE HAVE TO TRANSFER THE LIVER QUICKLY.
GRP
K-KLAK
NATSUME!
...
SSST

N-NATSUME...
WHAT HAVE YOU DONE?
YOU MUSTN'T WAKE HER UP.
IT'S TOO CRUEL!
YOU MUSTN'T WAKE HER UP!!
NATSUME...

I'M SORRY, PA.
I REALLY ...
I REALLY WANTED TO GO WITH YUTA.
YUTA'S LIKE ME.
WE'RE THE SAME.

NATSU-ME.
WHAT HAPPENED, NATSUME?
YOU'RE BLEEDING FROM YOUR STOMACH.
PA...
EVERY-THING WILL BE ALL RIGHT.
YOUR PA'S WITH YOU.
PA?
MPH
TMP TMP
THAT OLD MAN... HE WOULDN'T...
NGH!
KREE
PA?
WHAT'S WRONG, PA?
TMP TMP
YOU'RE ACTING FUNNY.

TMP
YOUR PA WILL BE WITH YOU ALL THE WAY.
YOU WON'T BE LONELY.
PA...
SWAY
STOP!!
TMP

LEAP
NATSU-ME!!
YUTA!!
NATSU-ME!
HUG
PA...
ALL RIGHT, PA...
SQUEEZE

...
NATSU-ME ...
NATSU-ME ...
...

BLINK
NATSU-ME...
HEH HEH. YOU DIDN'T THINK A LITTLE FALL OFF A CLIFF WOULD KILL ME, DID YOU?
IT WAS JUST THAT...
...I KINDA FELT SORRY FOR PA.
NATSUME... YOUR LIVER...
...

YUTA...
WHERE ARE YOU GOING?
NATSUME !!
I'LL FOLLOW YOU...
...WHEREVER YOU GO...

NATSUME
...
TMP
SHK

FLAP FLAP
FLAP
HER LAST RITES...
DON'T TOUCH HER.
I'LL TAKE CARE...
...OF NATSUME'S LAST RITES.

THE ASH PRINCESS / THE END

THANK YOU, YUTA, BUT...
...IT DOESN'T MATTER ANYMORE.
IT'S ALL MY FAULT.
THAT'S NOT TRUE, MISS AKIKO!
IT JUST DOESN'T MATTER ANYMORE.
FWOO
S-SOMEONE! COME QUICKLY!
MISS AKIKO AND MASTER SHINGO HAVE COMMITTED SUICIDE!!
MISS AKIKO...

Chapter 13: Mermaid's Gaze, Part 1

AS THE YEAR 1992 DRAWS NEAR...
...I TRUST ALL OUR VIEWERS ARE ENJOYING THIS NEW YEAR'S EVE.
FWOOOO
LEAVE.
NO MATTER HOW MANY TIMES YOU ASK...
...I DON'T KNOW WHAT BECAME OF THE DOLL.
I JUST DON'T KNOW!
IF YOU DON'T LEAVE THIS MINUTE, I'LL CALL THE POLICE.
THE POLICE ...
GOOD IDEA.
CHK

WHAT ARE YOU DOING?!
HERE YOU GO.
!
GRAB
JUST GIVING YOU A GOOD REASON TO CALL THE POLICE.
SHHK

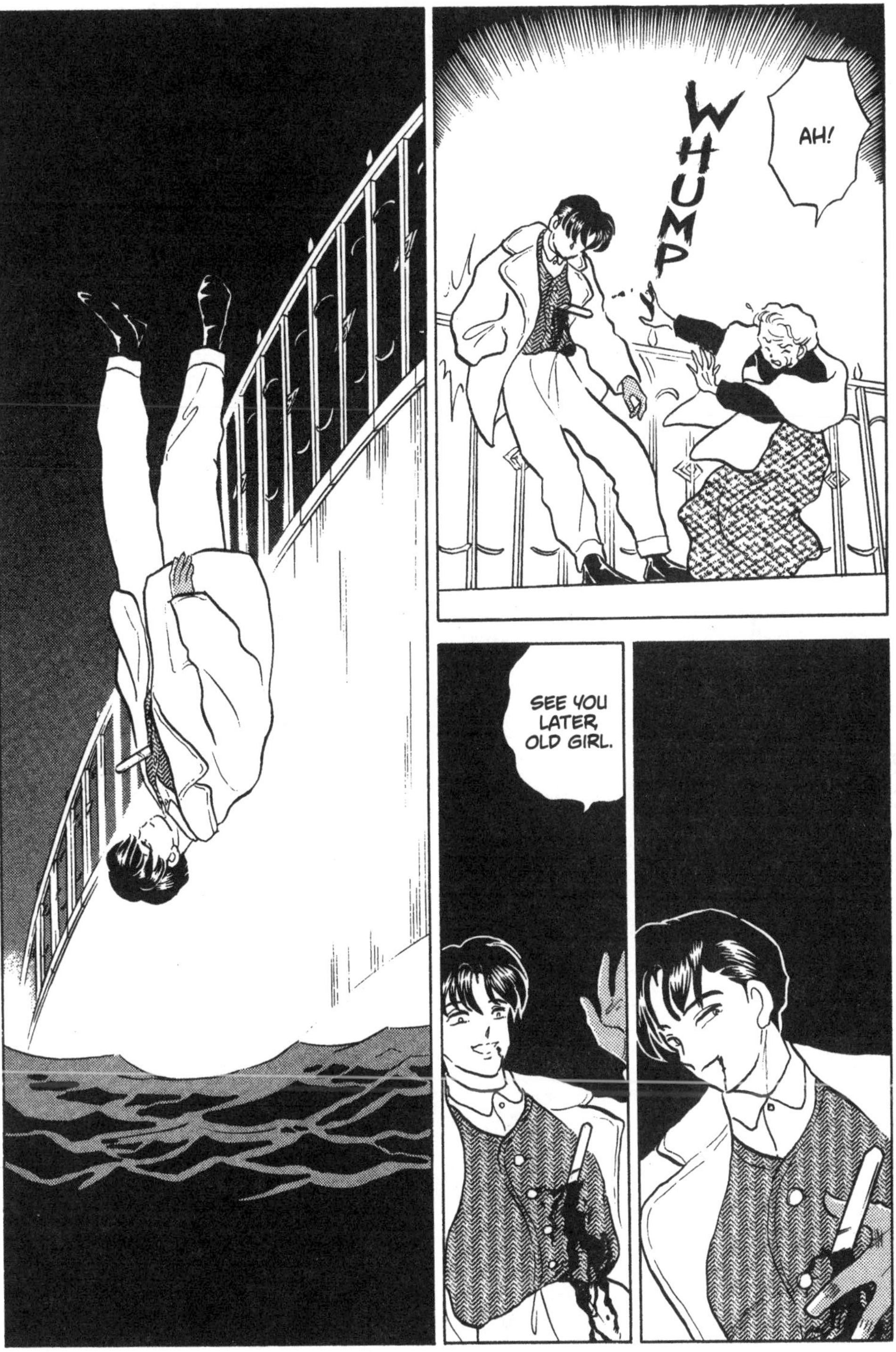
AH!
WHUMP
SEE YOU LATER, OLD GIRL.

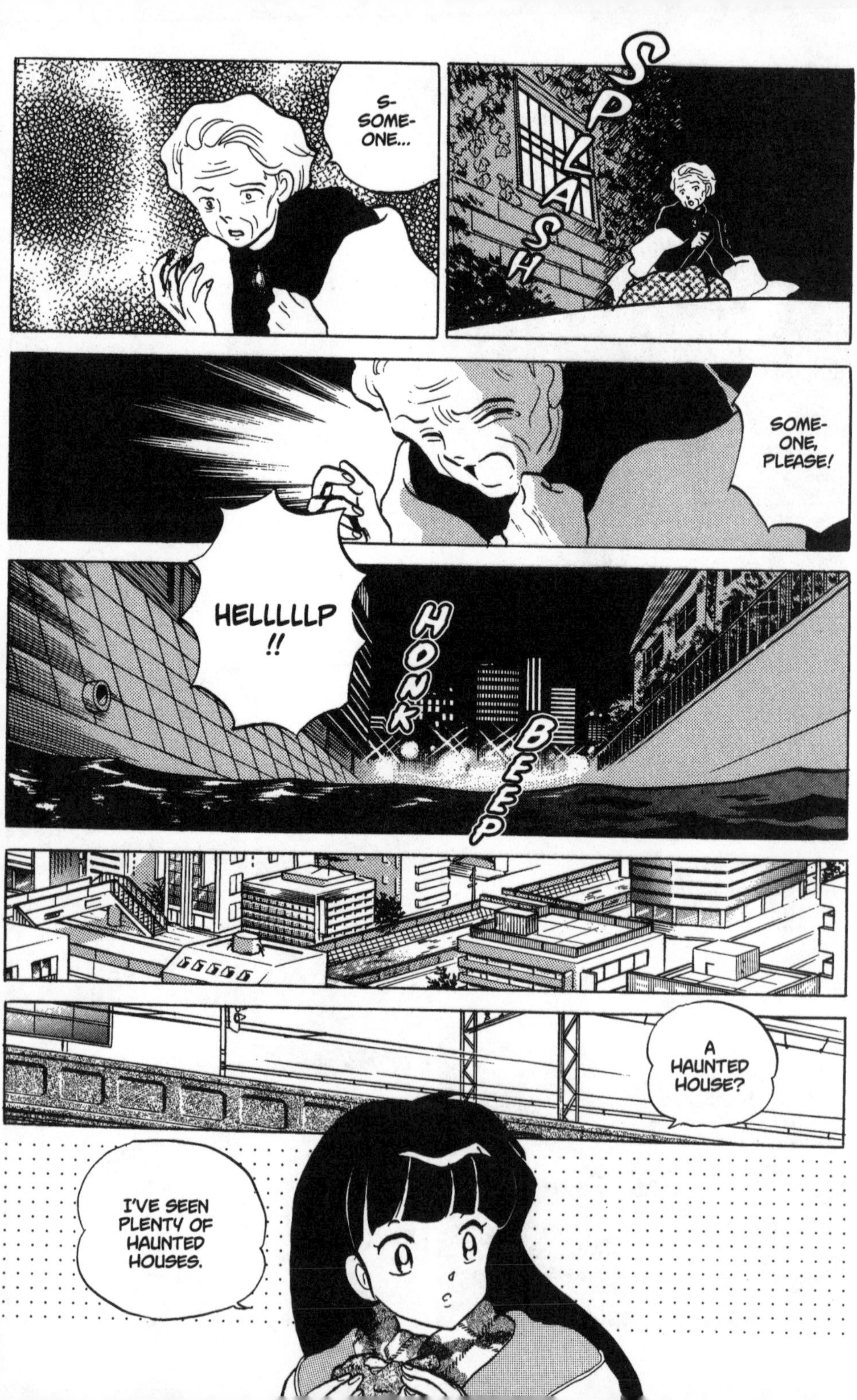
S-SOME-ONE...
SPLASH
SOME-ONE, PLEASE!
HELLLLLP!!
HONK
BEEP
A HAUNTED HOUSE?
I'VE SEEN PLENTY OF HAUNTED HOUSES.

KLAK KLAK KLAK
I'M NOT TALKING ABOUT A HAUNTED HOUSE AT A CARNIVAL, HONEY.
I'VE SEEN REAL ONES TOO–
THAT'S ENOUGH, MANA.
BEEEEP
EVERYONE IN THE AREA KNOWS THE GHOST STORIES ABOUT THE KIRYU MANSION.
KIRYU ...
IT'S AN OLD WESTERN-STYLE MANSION...
...BUILT IN THE 19TH CENTURY. ONLY AN OLD HOUSEKEEPER LIVES THERE.
BUT THEY SAY YOU CAN SEE A VERY YOUNG WOMAN SITTING BY THE WINDOW ALL DAY LONG.
A WOMAN?

SHE SITS THERE WITH A SAD EXPRESSION ON HER FACE. AS IF SHE'S...
... WAITING FOR SOMEONE.
BUT SHE DOESN'T MOVE AN INCH.
SOME SAY IT'S THE GHOST OF A GIRL WHO DIED IN THE HOUSE LONG AGO.
THE GHOST STORY I HEARD IS ABOUT A YOUNG **MAN**.
THE OLD WIDOW OF THE KIRYU MANSION CALLED THE POLICE...
...AND SAID SHE HAD KILLED A MAN.
BUT WHEN THE POLICE CHECKED IT OUT, THEY COULDN'T FIND A BODY.
AND IT DIDN'T HAPPEN JUST ONCE.
ACCORDING TO THE OLD WIDOW, THE MAN SHE CLAIMS TO HAVE KILLED...
...COMES BACK TO LIFE AND RETURNS AGAIN AND AGAIN.
IS THAT SO...

YUTA, ARE WE GOING...
...TO THAT HAUNTED HOUSE?
THEY SAY A MAN COMES BACK TO LIFE AGAIN AND AGAIN.
AREN'T YOU CURIOUS?
YOU THINK HE'S ONE OF US?
EITHER THAT, OR HE'S A GHOST.
BESIDES, THAT KIRYU MANSION THEY MENTIONED...
I ONCE WORKED THERE FOR A WHILE.
HMM.

MISS AKIKO AND MASTER SHINGO HAVE COMMITTED SUICIDE!!
A GHOST BY THE WINDOW...
FWOOO
YES?
MAY I HELP YOU?
UMM ...

WE CAME TO ASK ABOUT THE GHOST.
FWOO
...
WELL, I'M SORRY TO DISAPPOINT YOU...
...BUT THAT STORY-
HEY, OLD GIRL. I'M BACK.
TMP

OH, IF YOU'RE UPSET ABOUT THE OTHER DAY, DON'T BE.
AS YOU CAN SEE, I'M AS GOOD AS NEW.
GO AWAY!!
THAT MAN'S A DEVIL!
HE MEANS TO KILL US ALL!!
HMPH. THAT OLD BAG AGAIN.
SUGIKO ...

GO AWAY!!
KRASH
TSK, TSK. WHAT A WASTE.
CHASE HIM AWAY! CHASE HIM AWAY!
HM?
WHO ARE YOU?
JUST PASSING THROUGH.
I CAME TO ASK ABOUT SOME-THING.
ABOUT A MAN WHO COMES BACK TO LIFE.

HA.
IS THIS A HOBBY OF YOURS?
TAKE MY ADVICE AND GET OUT OF HERE, QUICK.
ONE WRONG MOVE...
...AND YOU MAY END UP BEING KILLED BY THIS OLD GIRL HERE.
KEN, WOULD YOU HURRY UP?
I'M FREEZ-ING!
BE RIGHT THERE!
GOTTA GO. DON'T WANT TO KEEP MY GIRLFRIEND WAITING.
...

LOOKS A BIT LIKE HER, DON'T YOU THINK?
WH-?
I MEAN, SHE'S NO MATCH FOR YOUR DOLL, BUT STILL...
J-JUST WHAT DO YOU-?
AW, IT'S ... ...NOTHING.
I JUST WANT YOU TO REMEMBER THIS GIRL'S FACE, THAT'S ALL.
RUN AWAY, CHILD!
YOU'LL BE KILLED!!
SHADDUP, YOU OLD BAG!
KICK
GROSS, WHAT'S WITH HER?
BEATS ME.

ARE YOU ALL RIGHT, MA'AM?
SUGIKO ...
IT'S MASTER SHINGO.
MASTER SHINGO HAS COME TO KILL US.
SHINGO ...
KLAT KLAT
FWOO
THAT'S BET-TER.
TH-THANK YOU.
I...I APPRECIATE YOUR HELP. BUT I'D LIKE YOU TO...
...LEAVE NOW.
TELL ME WHAT'S GOING ON.
PLEASE.

I'VE TOLD PEOPLE ABOUT THIS BEFORE, BUT NO ONE BELIEVES ME.
NOT THE NEIGHBORS...
NOT THE POLICE...
...
WHAT IS IT, YUTA?
YOU'VE GOT A SCARY LOOK ON YOUR FACE.
HM?
WELL ...
IT'S JUST THAT...
...THAT GUY MIGHT BE ...
...SOMEONE I KNOW.
WHAT ...?

IS... IS THAT TRUE?
WHO ON EARTH IS HE?
AND WHY...
WHY DOES HE COME BACK TO LIFE AGAIN AND AGAIN?!
FWOOO
HE FIRST APPEARED ABOUT A YEAR AGO.
I WANT YOU TO GIVE ME THE DOLL.
DOLL?
A VERY LARGE DOLL THAT HAS BEEN IN THE KIRYU FAMILY FOR MANY YEARS.

SUGIKO ...
SUGIKO HAS WORKED IN THIS HOUSE FOR YEARS.
APPARENTLY SHE WAS HERE BRIEFLY AS A CHILD TOO.
THEN AFTER LOSING HER FAMILY, SHE CAME BACK HERE.
SHE SAYS THE DOLL WAS HERE...
...WHEN SHE WAS A CHILD, BEFORE THE WAR...
...SO IT MUST BE VERY OLD.
WHEN MY HUSBAND WAS STILL ALIVE, IT WAS KEPT IN AN UNUSED ROOM.
AT ANY RATE, IT WAS A MAGNIFICENT DOLL...
...SO IT SEEMED A SHAME TO KEEP IT SHUT UP IN A DARK ROOM.
AFTER MY HUSBAND PASSED AWAY, AND SUGIKO AND I WERE THE ONLY ONES LEFT...
...WE PLACED IT BY THE SUNNIEST WINDOW IN THE HOUSE.
HMPH. SO IT WASN'T A GHOST AFTER ALL.

IT WAS AFTER THAT MAN FIRST APPEARED...
...THAT SUGIKO BECAME LIKE THIS.
IT'S A GHOST.
IT'S THE GHOST OF MASTER SHINGO!
SUGIKO!
WHAT DO YOU MEAN?!
AT FIRST I HAD NO IDEA WHAT SHE WAS TALKING ABOUT.
BUT...
SUGIKO HID THE DOLL AWAY SOMEWHERE.
SO I TOLD THE MAN...
I CAN'T GIVE YOU THE DOLL.
THEN ONE DAY...
WHO'S THERE ?!
RATTLE
...THAT MAN BROKE INTO THE HOUSE.
GIVE ME THE DOLL!
I WAS AFRAID. I DIDN'T KNOW WHAT I WAS DOING.

A... AAAHH!
WHEN I CAME TO THE NEXT MORNING...
...THE MAN'S CORPSE WAS GONE. THE BLOOD ON THE FLOOR HAD BEEN COMPLETELY CLEANED AWAY.
ARE YOU SURE YOU WEREN'T DREAMING, MA'AM?
IT-IT'S THE TRUTH. YOU'LL SEE IF YOU CHECK CAREFULLY ENOUGH.
GOOD AFTER-NOON.
WHAT'S ALL THE FUSS ABOUT?
THE MAN WHO WAS SUPPOSED TO BE DEAD...
...REAPPEARED AS IF NOTHING HAD EVER HAPPENED!

IT'S ALL SO ABSURD.
I...
I WONDER IF I'M THE ONE WHO'S GONE MAD.
MA'AM ...
LET ME SHOW YOU SOMETHING INTERESTING.
TMP
HERE YOU GO.
SINCE WHEN HAVE YOU STARTED READING MY MIND?
GRP
SHK
AH!
WIPE
TH... THE WOUND ...
IT'S DISAP-PEARED!

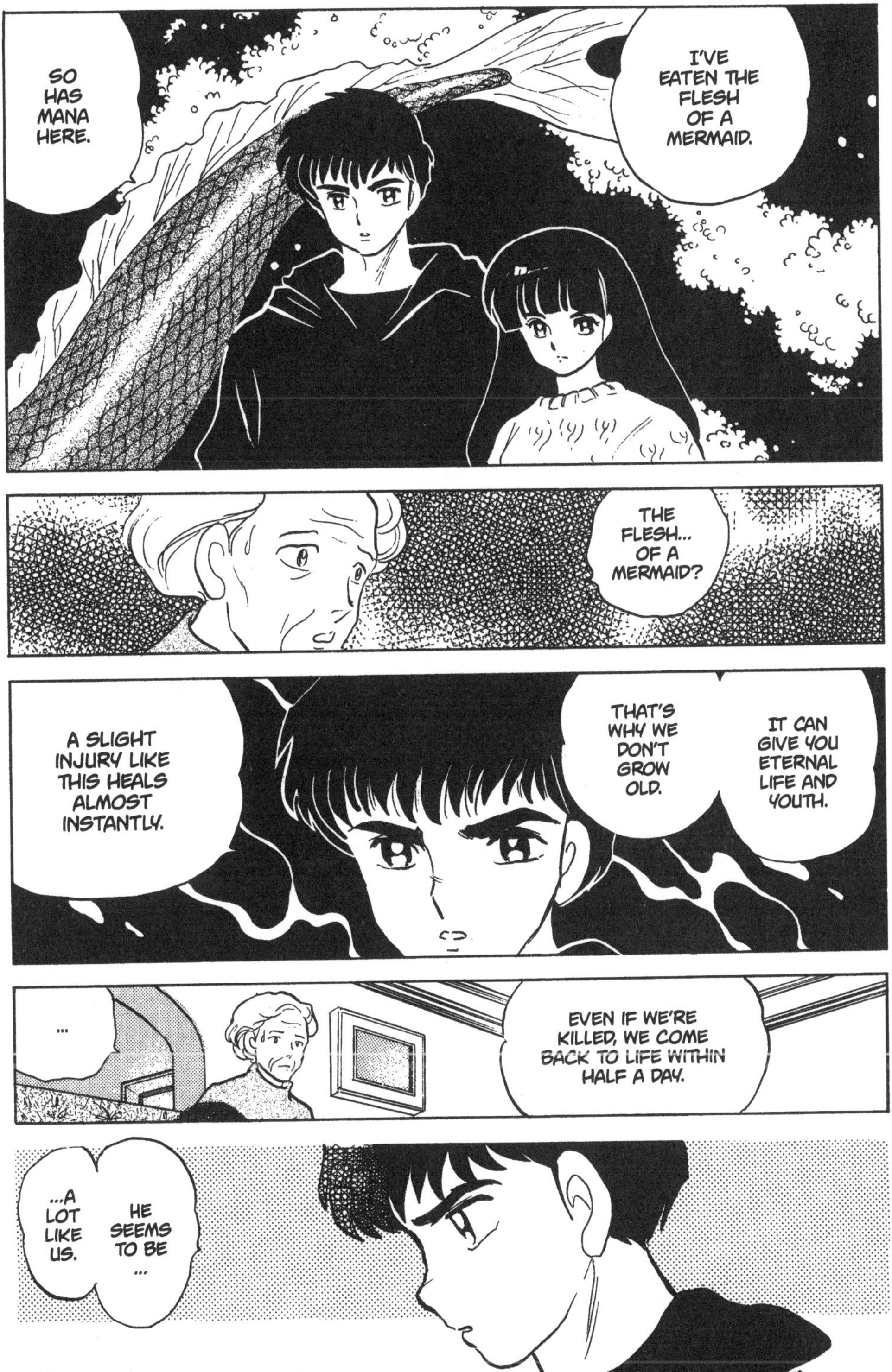
I'VE EATEN THE FLESH OF A MERMAID.
SO HAS MANA HERE.
THE FLESH... OF A MERMAID?
IT CAN GIVE YOU ETERNAL LIFE AND YOUTH.
THAT'S WHY WE DON'T GROW OLD.
A SLIGHT INJURY LIKE THIS HEALS ALMOST INSTANTLY.
EVEN IF WE'RE KILLED, WE COME BACK TO LIFE WITHIN HALF A DAY.
...
HE SEEMS TO BE ...
...A LOT LIKE US.

YAKICHI'S DAUGHTER WAS FOUND FLOATING IN THE RIVER.
MASTER SHINGO AGAIN...
SHH!
I WAS WORKING IN THIS HOUSE.
THIS WAS AT THE VERY BEGINNING OF THIS CENTURY, JUST BEFORE THE RUSSO-JAPANESE WAR.
SHINGO, PLEASE...
YOU MUSTN'T DO THESE THINGS ANYMORE.
SHUT UP!
IT'S ALL YOUR FAULT ANYWAY!
WHAP
MISS AKIKO ...
YUTA...
PLEASE...
DON'T MENTION THIS TO ANYONE.
IT'S MY FAULT MY BROTHER IS LIKE THIS.
MISS AKIKO ...

THE ELDEST SON OF THIS MANSION, SHINGO, WAS AN ANIMAL.
HE WOULD SET FIRES FOR THE FUN OF IT.
HE WOULD BEAT WOMEN AND CHILDREN TO WITHIN AN INCH OF THEIR LIVES.
BUT NO MATTER WHAT HE DID...
...HIS FAMILY WOULD USE ITS INFLUENCE TO HUSH IT UP.
AND AKIKO, THE OLDER SISTER OF THAT MONSTER...
...ALWAYS KEPT HIM FROM BEING PUNISHED.
MISS AKIKO ALWAYS LOOKED SAD.
AND JUST WHEN SHE BECAME ENGAGED AND WAS FINALLY ON THE VERGE OF HAPPINESS...
...HER FIANCÉ WAS POISONED AND DIED.
THEY NEVER FOUND OUT WHO THE MURDERER WAS, BUT...
AKIKO.
DON'T GO OFF AND GET MARRIED.
IF YOU LEAVE, WHO WILL KEEP ME FROM GETTING PUNISHED?

MISS AKIKO ...
IF THERE'S ANYTHING I CAN DO FOR YOU...
THANK YOU, YUTA.
BUT IT DOESN'T MATTER ANYMORE.
IT'S ALL MY FAULT.
THAT'S NOT TRUE, MISS AKIKO!
IT JUST DOESN'T MATTER ANYMORE.
S-SOMEONE! COME QUICKLY!
MISS AKIKO AND MASTER SHINGO HAVE COMMITTED SUICIDE!!
WHEN THE FUNERALS FOR THE TWO WERE OVER...
...I LEFT THE KIRYU MANSION.
TMP TMP TMP
LOCK HIM UP!
LOCK UP MASTER SHINGO!!
HE'LL KILL US!
WE'LL ALL BE KILLED!!

IT'S SUGIKO AGAIN!
FWOO
THE BASE-MENT ...?
SUGIKO ?!
A PRISON CELL...
MUMBLE
PLEASE, SUGIKO ...
OPEN THE DOOR.
MUMBLE
I WAS THE ONE WHO LET HIM OUT.
WE HAVE TO LOCK HIM UP AGAIN.

ISN'T THIS GREAT, YUTA? A FREE PLACE TO SLEEP.
DOESN'T ANYTHING EVER FAZE YOU?
ARE WE GOING TO STAY HERE LONG?
IF THAT'S THE SHINGO I KNOW...
...AND HE'S EATEN THE FLESH OF A MERMAID, WE CAN'T JUST WALK AWAY.
"IF" HE'S SHINGO ...?
HE **LOOKS** LIKE SHINGO ...
...EXCEPT FOR ONE THING.

SHINGO ...
...HAD NO RIGHT EYE.
FWOO
NO!!
SHF SHF SHF

SHF SHF
STOP!!
FWOO
YOU'RE AN UNLUCKY GIRL...
YOU LOOKED TOO MUCH LIKE MY SISTER.

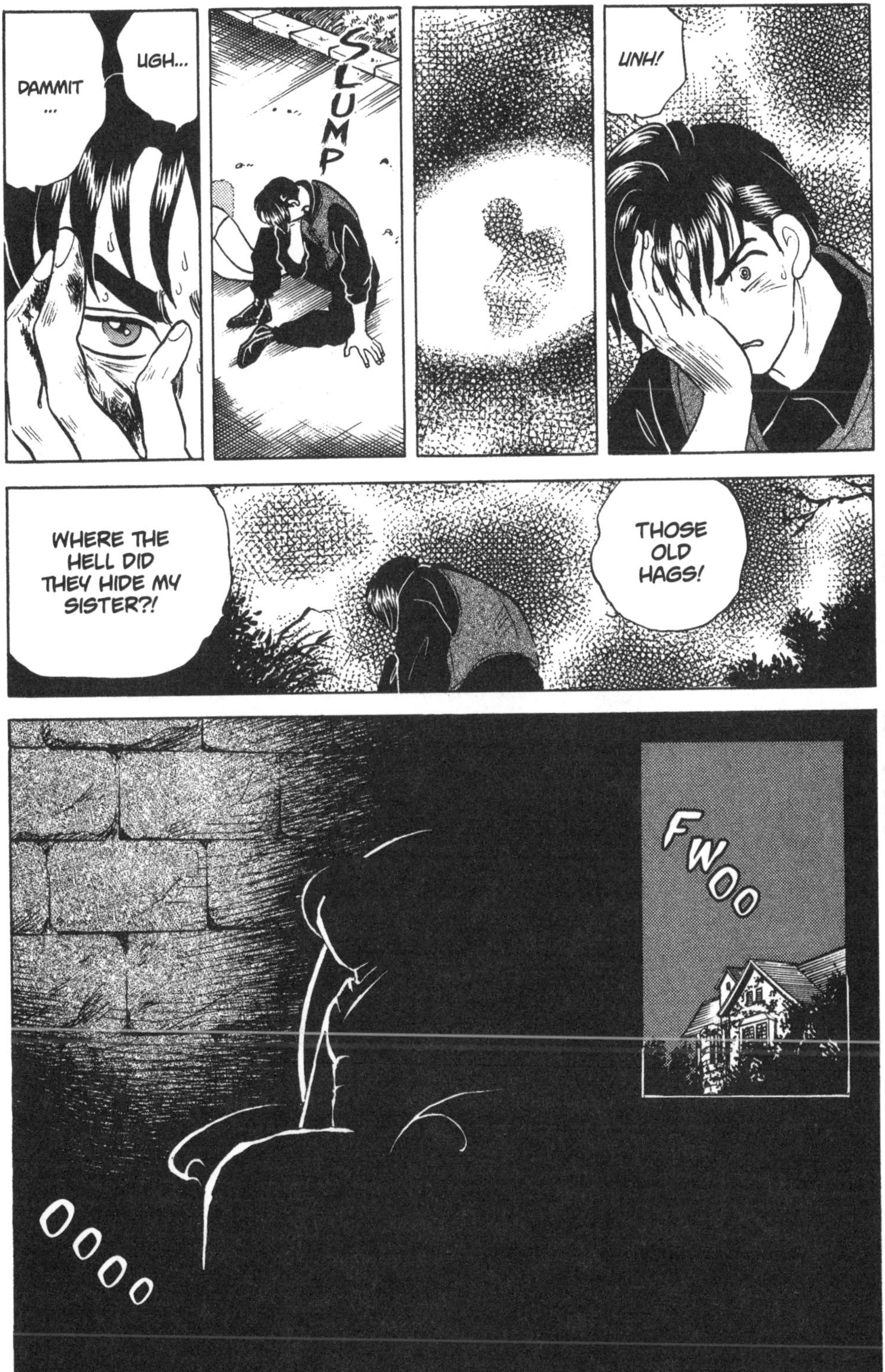
UNH!
SLUMP
UGH...
DAMMIT ...
THOSE OLD HAGS!
WHERE THE HELL DID THEY HIDE MY SISTER?!
FWOO
OOOO

...
OHO!
YOU KIDS STILL HANGING AROUND?
CHIRP

SAY, YOU'RE PRETTY CUTE.
WHAT'S YOUR NAME? HOW OLD ARE YOU?
I'M NOT TALKING TO YOU.
YUTA TOLD ME YOU'RE DANGEROUS.
DASH
YUTA...?
OH, THAT GUY...
YOU SAY HE'S AFTER YOUR DOLL.
WHAT ON EARTH...
...WOULD HE WANT WITH A DOLL?
I CAN'T IMAGINE.
SIZZLE
THE DOLL ...
THAT POOR THING ...
...
AND NOW THE NEWS ...
LAST NIGHT ...

FOREST PARK SLAYING
(22)
... A WOMAN WAS FOUND STABBED TO DEATH IN FOREST PARK.
THE 22-YEAR-OLD WOMAN WAS A RESIDENT OF...
KLAT
"I JUST WANT YOU TO REMEMBER..."
"...THIS GIRL'S FACE, THAT'S ALL."
MORNING MA'AM!
SEEN THE PAPER YET?
Y-Y-YOU-!!

Y... YOU DIDN'T...
THE POLICE HAVE NO LEADS IN THE CASE AT THIS TIME.
AH, THEY'RE TALKING ABOUT IT RIGHT NOW.
DASH
CLENCH
WELL ...
I JUST GOT KIND OF LONELY, YOU KNOW?
IF I FIND ANOTHER GIRL WHO LOOKS LIKE THAT...
...I'LL COME BACK TO DELIVER THE PAPER AGAIN.
HOLD IT.
GRP

DO I LOOK ...
... FAMILIAR TO YOU?
WHAT'S YOUR PROBLEM?
YOU HAVE SOME KIND OF GRUDGE AGAINST ME?
FLICK
LET GO.
SLICE
AHH !!
WHAT DO YOU THINK YOU'RE DOING?!
Y- YUTA ...
I'M AFRAID THERE ARE TOO MANY PEOPLE WHO HAVE GRUDGES AGAINST ME.
I CAN'T KEEP TRACK OF THEM ALL.
FWOO
KLAT
A POOR INNOCENT GIRL...
WHY ...?

SUGIKO ...
WHERE DID YOU HIDE THAT DOLL?
LET'S JUST GIVE HIM THE DOLL!
AT THIS RATE ...
IF WE GIVE IT TO HIM...
...WE'LL ALL BE KILLED!
IT'LL BE OKAY.
I'LL MAKE SURE NOTHING HAPPENS TO ANYONE.
NOW, LISTEN TO ME ...
WHY DON'T YOU SHOW US THE DOLL?
...
DO YOU MEAN IT?
KLATTER
KREEE

SOME TIME AFTER MASTER SHINGO ESCAPED ...
...WE DUG A NEW CELLAR.
OH, MY... I DIDN'T KNOW THERE WAS ANOTHER CELLAR.
TUMP
WE USED IT AS AN AIR RAID SHELTER IN THE SECOND WORLD WAR.
KLANG
!
KREE
RMMBL

AH...!

THANK YOU, YUTA.
BUT IT DOESN'T MATTER ANYMORE.
IT'S ALL MY FAULT.
AH...
MISS ...
...AKIKO ...!
WHAT ?!
A CORPSE ?

SHE'S COVERED WITH WAX.
IS SHE DEAD?
D-DON'T BE RIDICU-LOUS.
IT'S BEEN IN THE FAMILY FOR DECADES.
IF IT WERE A CORPSE, IT WOULD HAVE ROTTED LONG AGO.
THE FLESH OF A MERMAID...
IF THE POISON AKIKO AND SHINGO USED...
...WAS THE FLESH OF A MERMAID...
...THEN THIS IS MISS AKIKO'S CORPSE... PRESERVED FOR ETERNITY!
WHAT DOES HE INTEND TO DO WITH THIS...?

SHINGO.
WHAT WE'VE JUST EATEN...
...IS POISON.
W-WHAT DID YOU JUST SAY??!
IT'S A POISON THAT'S BEEN IN THE FAMILY FOR GENERATIONS.
THEY SAY IT'S PAINLESS.
IT'S ALL RIGHT.
I'LL BE WITH YOU ALL THE WAY, SHINGO.

SHINGO!
YOUR SISTER IS DEAD!
IT...
IT SHOULD HAVE BEEN YOU INSTEAD!
KLANG
DAMMIT, FATHER!
LET ME OUT OF HERE!
HMPH. SOME POISON.
WHAT THE HELL DID SHE FEED ME, ANYWAY?
HMM. THAT GUY YUTA...
DO I LOOK FAMILIAR?

HMM...
HM?
KEEP AWAY FROM MY SISTER, YOU WORM.
WHY DON'T YOU TRY TO BECOME A DECENT HUMAN BEING INSTEAD?
I TELL YOU, YUTA...
YOU'RE REALLY SOMETHING.
SLASH
FWUP
CAN... CAN IT BE...?

IS THAT REALLY...
...THE YUTA I KILLED THAT TIME?
WAIT A MINUTE. THEN THAT MEANS...
...I'M NOT THE ONLY ONE WHO'S IMMORTAL.
A GUY WHO'S IMMORTAL HAS SHOWN UP AT THE HOUSE WHERE MY SISTER IS.
WELL, WELL...
TWO BIRDS WITH ONE STONE...
FWOO

ANYWAY, THE TWO OF YOU...
...SHOULD GET AWAY FROM THIS HOUSE.
B-BUT IF WE JUST GIVE HIM THE DOLL...
...
NO. I DON'T WANT TO GIVE HIM THE DOLL.
...
FZZT
A POWER FAILURE?
SHH!

FWOO
RATTLE
KREE
HE'S HERE?!
IT'S CRAMPED ...
...BUT YOU'RE SAFER HERE.
LET'S GO, YUTA.
YOU GET IN THERE TOO!
NUDGE
WHA-?!

LISTEN TO ME, MANA.
IT'S YOUR JOB TO PROTECT THESE WOMEN.
YUTA.
YOU WERE IN LOVE WITH THAT GIRL, AKIKO, WEREN'T YOU?
WHA-
WHY ASK SOMETHING LIKE THAT AT A TIME LIKE THIS?!
ANY-WAY...
...JUST TO WARN YOU, MA'AM, YOUR HOUSE MAY GET A BIT MESSY.
DASH
WE'RE GOING TO BE KILLED...
QUIET DOWN, SUGIKO.
TREMBLE
FWOOO
RATTLE
KRAK

SHINGO IS A HOMICIDAL MANIAC.
AS LONG AS HE LIVES, HE'LL KEEP ON KILLING.
KLAK
IF HE'S BECOME IMMORTAL...
...THEN I'LL HAVE TO TAKE CARE OF HIM MYSELF.
CINCH
KREE

JUST WAIT, AKIKO.
I'M COMING.
KREEEE

FWOOO
FWOOO

Chapter 14: Mermaid's Gaze, Part 2

FWOO
KREE
YO.
COME ON OUT.
I KNOW YOU'RE THERE.
KREEK

VSH
WHOA!
KRASH
TMP TMP TMP
UP THERE, HM?
HEH HEH HEH.
BLAM
A GUN?!
SHFF

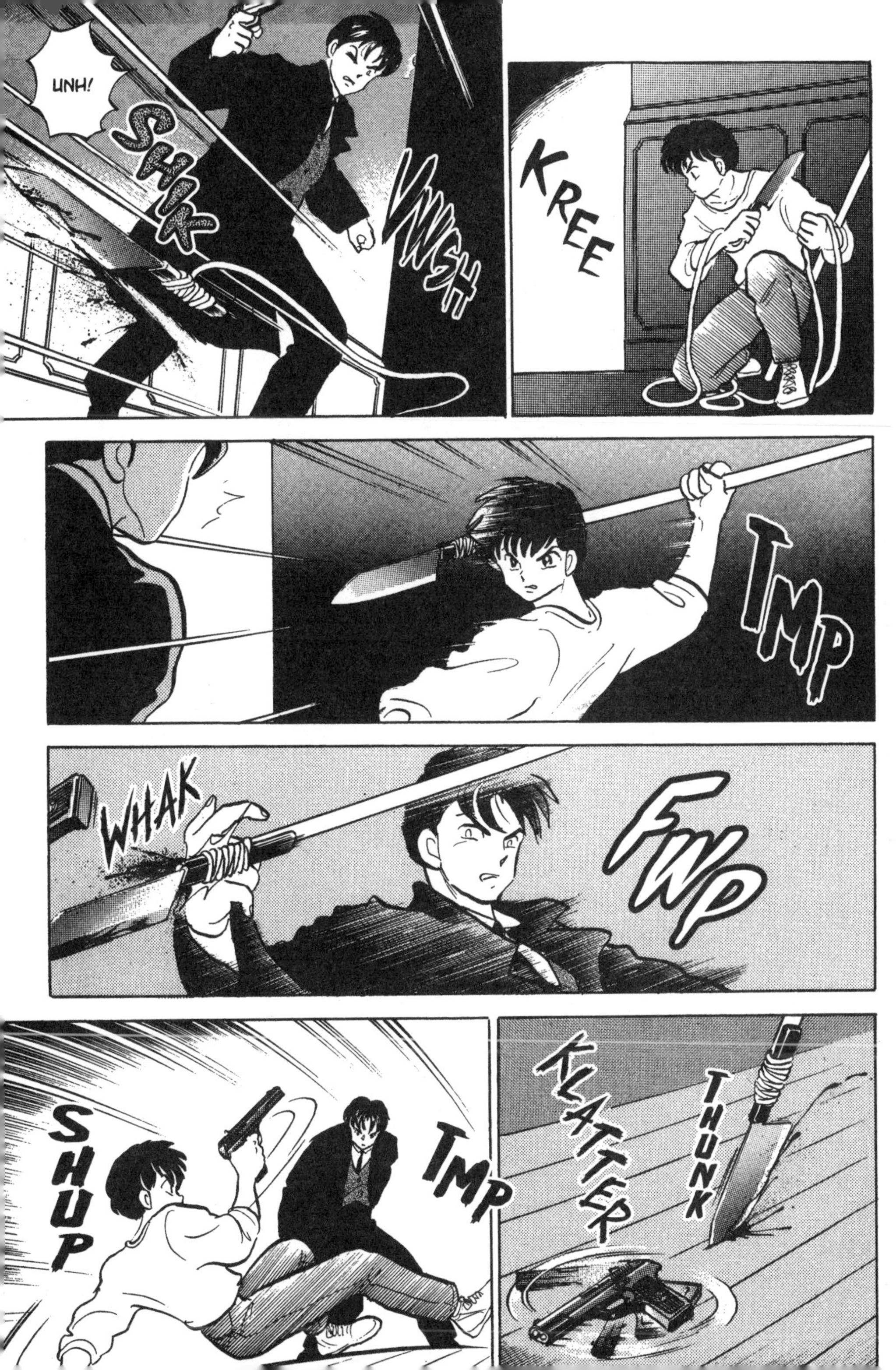
KREE
UNH!
SHK
VWSH
TMP
FWP
WHAK
THUNK
KLATTER
TMP
SHUP

YUTA.
BEEN A CENTURY OR SO, HASN'T IT?
SO THEN...
...YOU ARE THAT SHINGO.
FWOO
RATTLE
MASTER SHINGO IS GOING TO KILL US ALL...
SUGIKO, SHH!
IT'S SO QUIET ALL OF A SUDDEN...
THEY MUST HAVE MOVED UPSTAIRS.

W-WE SHOULD USE THIS OPPORTUNITY TO CALL THE POLICE.
THERE'S NO POINT.
NEITHER YUTA NOR SHINGO IS GOING TO DIE.
THERE'S NOTHING FOR THE POLICE TO DO.
HEY, I JUST CAME TO ASK SOME QUESTIONS.
DON'T GIVE ME THAT.
YUTA.
TELL ME WHY I DON'T DIE.
SEE? THAT WOUND IS GONE ALREADY.
WHA-?

YOU MEAN... YOU DON'T KNOW...
...ABOUT MERMAID FLESH?
MERMAID FLESH?
IT CAN MAKE YOU IMMORTAL.
YOU NEVER AGE AND YOU NEVER DIE.
BUT...
...THE FLESH OF THE MERMAID TRANSFORMS YOUR BODY COMPLETELY.
MOST PEOPLE DON'T SURVIVE THE TRANSFORMATION.
THEY DIE.
THE WAY MISS AKIKO—YOUR SISTER—DID.
...

SHINGO.
WHAT WE'VE JUST EATEN...
...IS POISON.
SO THAT'S WHAT IT WAS.
IT'S A POISON THAT'S BEEN IN THE FAMILY FOR GENERATIONS.
SO THAT DAMN SISTER OF MINE...
...PLANNED TO KILL HERSELF AND ME WITHOUT EVEN KNOW-ING WHAT THE POISON WAS?
HA!
THAT GIRL WAS EVEN MORE OF A NUISANCE THAN I THOUGHT.
NOT ONLY DID SHE SCREW UP MY LIFE-
YOU...
YOU BASTARD!

YOU WANT A FIGHT? IS THAT IT?!
VSH
!
K-BLAM
DAMN !!
PAK PAK
SHIK

WHUMP
DMP DMP DMP
MOM, SOMETHING'S GOING ON NEXT DOOR.
PAY NO ATTENTION, DEAR.
WHENEVER THE POLICE SHOW UP, IT TURNS OUT TO BE NOTHING AT ALL.
THEY PROBABLY JUST HAVE THE TV ON LOUD.
YOU... YOU WERE THE ONE WHO DROVE AKIKO TO THIS—!
IT DOESN'T MATTER ANYMORE, YUTA.
IT'S ALL MY FAULT.

EVER SINCE SHINGO WAS SMALL, HE... HE LIKED TO KILL ANIMALS WITH KNIVES AND THINGS.
ONCE, WHEN I TRIED TO STOP HIM...
SO THAT'S HOW IT HAPPENED...
"AND BECAUSE I PUT OUT SHINGO'S EYE..."
"...HE HAS ALWAYS BLAMED HIS PROBLEMS ON THAT..."
SHINGO!
I'M GOING TO DO WHAT I SHOULD HAVE DONE LONG AGO!
NO, FATHER! PLEASE SPARE HIM!
IT WASN'T AKIKO'S FAULT.
YOU WERE ROTTEN TO BEGIN WITH.

YOU...
...ARE COMPLETELY BEYOND REDEMPTION.
HEH.
WE HAVE TO LOCK MASTER SHINGO UP AGAIN.
WE HAVE TO LOCK HIM UP!!
BAM
AH!!
WAIT!!
TMP TMP TMP TMP TMP
!!

GRP
COME BACK!
K-BLAM
AH!!
THUD
FWP
WUMP
MANA !!

SNATCH
SLASH
!
UNGH!
SHUNK
YUTA!
YUTA ...
S...
STAY BACK, MANA.
SWAY

SHUP
NHN...
?!
TELL ME, YUTA...

WHAT DOES SOMEONE WHO'S EATEN THE FLESH OF A MERMAID HAVE TO DO TO DIE?
W...
WHAT...?
I MEAN, A SUREFIRE WAY TO DIE.
YOU SEE, MY SISTER...
...IS ALIVE.

FWOOO
WHAT ARE YOU TALKING ABOUT?
ALIVE?
THIS RIGHT EYE OF MINE...

...IS
THE REAL
THING. IT'S
ALIVE.
WHERE
DO YOU
THINK I
GOT IT
FROM?
HE TOOK
THE
DOLL'S
EYE.
THE
POOR
THING...
!

THAT'S RIGHT. AFTER AKIKO TRIED TO KILL US BOTH...
...MY POOR OLD MAN LOST HIS DARLING DAUGHTER AND WAS LEFT WITH ONLY HIS DESPISED SON...
YOU WERE THE ONE WHO SHOULD HAVE DIED!!
MY FATHER KILLED ME, AND I WAS BURIED WITH MY SISTER.
BUT, WOULDN'T YOU KNOW IT? I CAME BACK TO LIFE.
SINCE I CAME BACK TO LIFE...
...I GUESS MY OLD MAN THOUGHT SHE MIGHT TOO.
SO HE DUG MY SISTER UP.

SHE DIDN'T COME BACK TO LIFE, BUT SHE DIDN'T ROT EITHER.
HE COULDN'T BEAR THE THOUGHT OF BURYING OR CREMATING HER.
SO MY SISTER AND I BECAME THE UGLY FAMILY SECRET.
A FEW DECADES LATER...
...SUGIKO, THE OLD BAG SITTING THERE, WAS GIVEN THE JOB OF FEEDING ME.
PLEASE, SUGIKO.
LET ME OUT.

THAT FOOL SUGIKO DID JUST WHAT I TOLD HER TO.
TH-THE KEY...
TMP
THIS IS ALL YOUR FAULT...
DAMN YOU!!
WUP

HE TOOK...
...THE DOLL'S EYE...
YOU TWISTED SON OF A-
AFTER I ESCAPED...
...AS I SAT STARING AT MY SISTER'S PRETTY EYE, I THOUGHT...
...MAYBE THIS THING STILL **WORKS**.
AH...
I CAN SEE ...
BUT THIS EYE...
...CAME WITH SOMETHING I DIDN'T BARGAIN FOR.

IT CAME WITH ME.
I WAS THE LAST THING MY SISTER SAW.
THE IMAGE OF ME, REACHING TO RIP MY SISTER'S EYE FROM HER HEAD...
...WAS BURNED INTO HER EYE.
I LOOK LIKE A DEMON!

FOR SOME REASON ...
...EVERY TIME I TRY TO KILL SOMEONE...
...THAT IMAGE APPEARS TO ME.
MY SISTER WAS ALIVE.
SHE WAS WATCHING ME.
EVEN NOW... SHE'S WATCHING ME.
TELL ME, YUTA!
HOW CAN I KILL MY SISTER ONCE AND FOR ALL?!
MISS AKIKO...

...SITTING IN THE DARK ALL THESE YEARS...
WHAT IS IT YOU'VE BEEN WATCHING?
IT MUST HAVE BEEN SO PAINFUL.
IT MUST BE PAINFUL STILL.
MANA, LEND ME...
...YOUR SHOUL-DER.
LET'S GO.
I'LL TAKE YOU TO AKIKO.

KREE
FWOOOO
KLANG
KREE

FWOOO

GULP

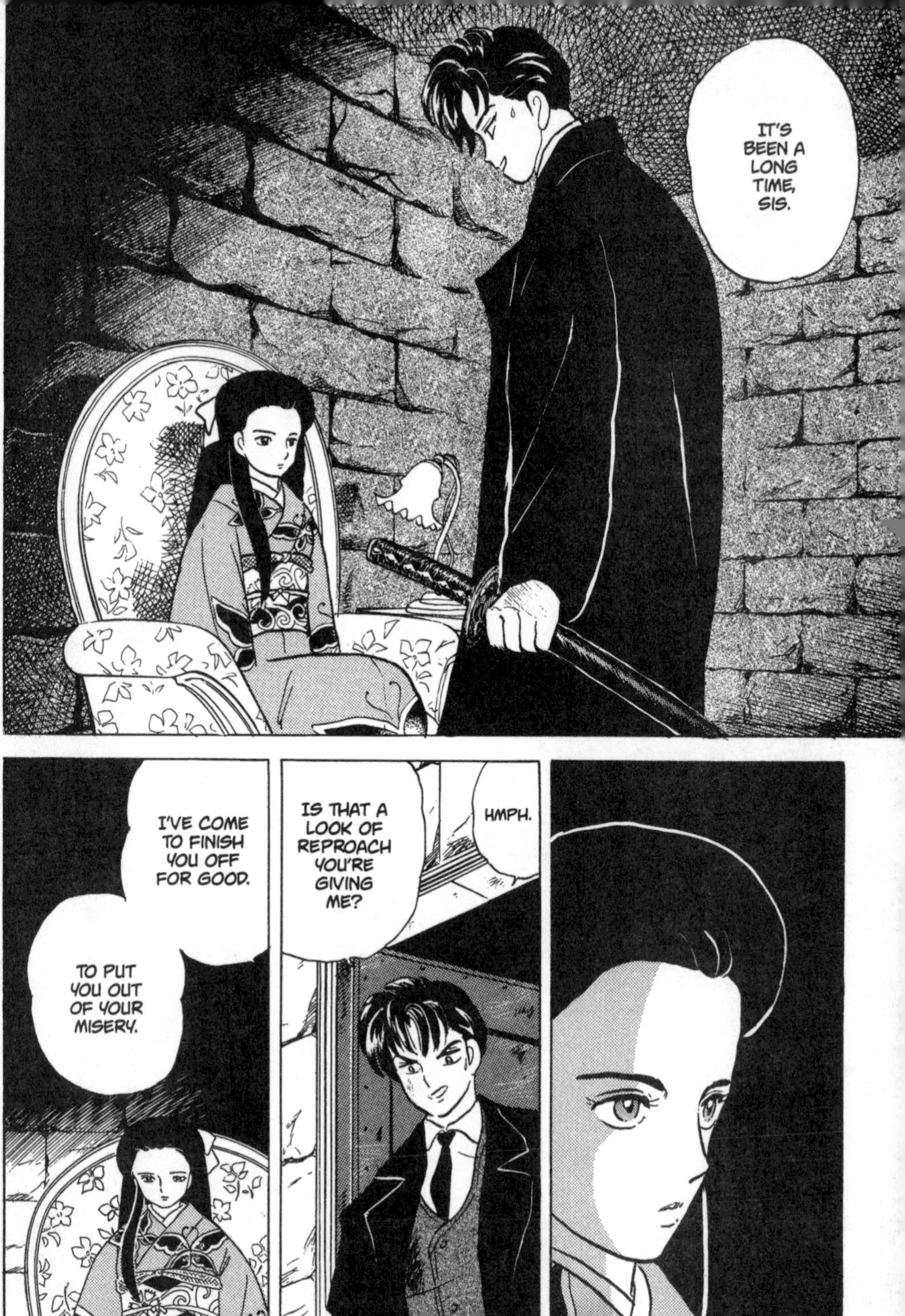
IT'S BEEN A LONG TIME, SIS.
I'VE COME TO FINISH YOU OFF FOR GOOD.
TO PUT YOU OUT OF YOUR MISERY.
IS THAT A LOOK OF REPROACH YOU'RE GIVING ME?
HMPH.

WELL, YUTA?
HOW DO I DO IT?
GIVE ME THE SWORD.
I'LL DO IT.
YUTA ...

AKIKO'S SPIRIT WILL NEVER REST...
...IF SHE'S KILLED BY THE LIKES OF SHINGO.
HMPH.
IT MAKES NO DIFFERENCE TO ME.
JUST AS LONG AS MY SISTER LEAVES THIS WORLD FOR GOOD.
FWOO

DON'T WORRY, MISS AKIKO.
I'LL TAKE CARE OF SHINGO.
YOU CAN REST NOW.

THAK

FWMP

SO IT'S FINALLY OVER.
NO.
IT'S NOT OVER YET.
SHINGO!
IT'S YOUR TURN!!

SLASH
UNH!
K-BLAM

SWAY
TMP
DASH
K-BLAM
UNGH!
SLASH
FWUMP
TUMP

YUTA!
GIVE ME THE SWORD!
STAY BACK!
I'M GOING TO FINISH THIS GUY OFF...
...WITH MY OWN HANDS.
HA!
YOU THINK I'M GOING TO ROLL OVER AND DIE NOW?
WHEN...

...I'M FINALLY FREE OF MY SISTER?!
K-BLAM
THAK
EAT THAT, YOU-
...

IT'S STILL THERE...

IT'S STILL THERE!
MISH
?
SLUMP

SHK
AKIKO...
AREN'T YOU DEAD YET?
WELL ?!
FWUP
SHATTER

YOU MEAN...
...I HAVE TO GO ON LOOKING AT MY WRETCHED SELF...
...FOR ETERNITY?

DAMN.
SHA
ALL RIGHT, AKIKO.
ALL RIGHT.
TUP
THAK

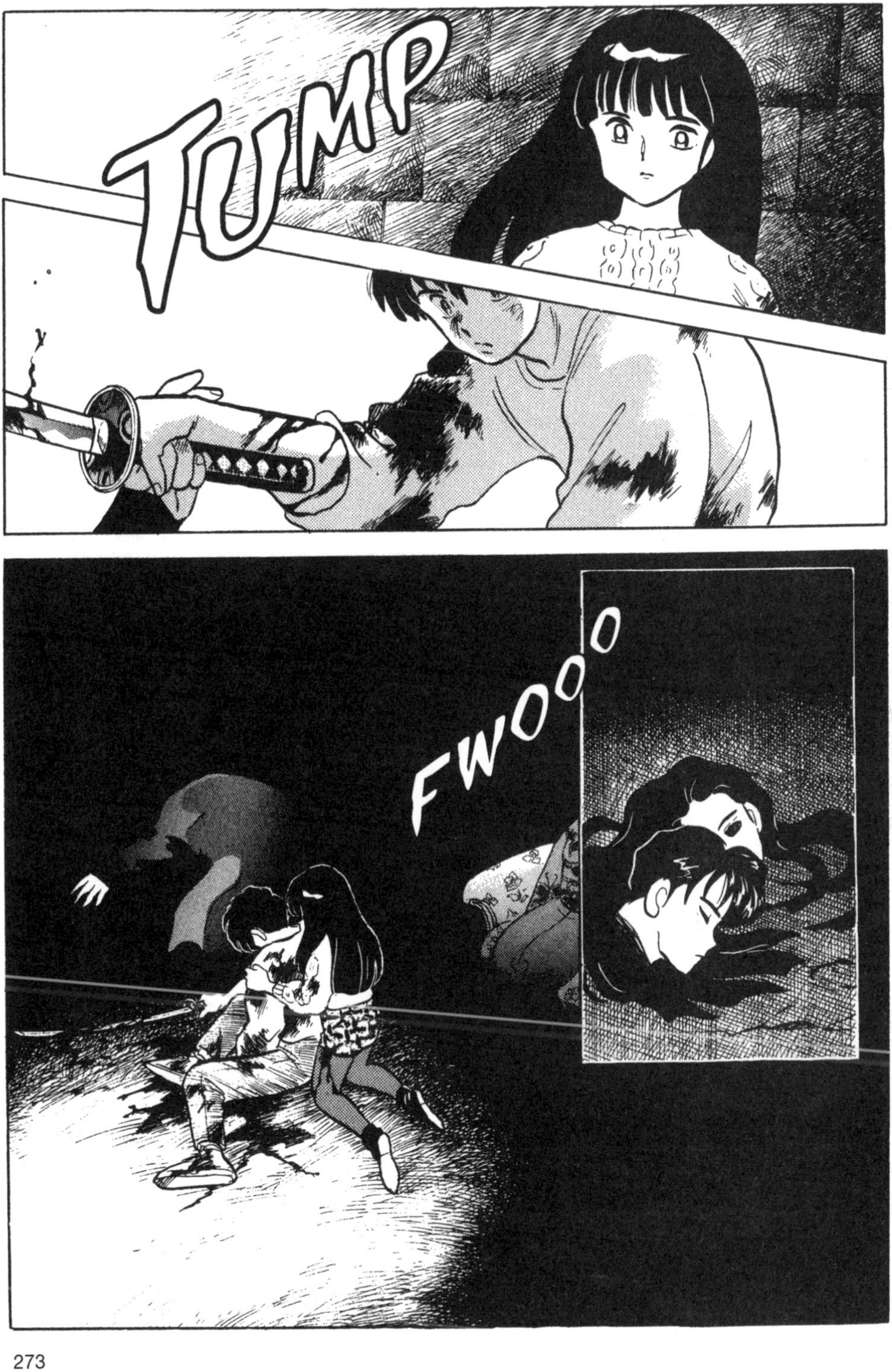
TUMP
FWOOO

THE DOLL HAS...
...TAKEN MASTER SHINGO FAR, FAR AWAY...
HE WON'T EVER COME BACK. I PROMISE.
DO YOU UNDERSTAND, SUGIKO?
Y...
YES, MA'AM.
KLAK
KLAK

KLAK KLAK
YUTA.
HM?
I DON'T THINK AKIKO WAS ALIVE.
I THINK SHINGO WAS SEEING A GHOST.
...
I'LL BUY THAT.
IF ONLY BECAUSE IT'S EASIER TO THINK THAT.

HEY...
MANA... COULD IT BE THAT...
...YOU'RE TRYING TO MAKE ME FEEL BETTER?
GEE, YOU DON'T HAVE TO DO THAT.
IT'S NO PROBLEM.

Mermaid's Gaze / The End

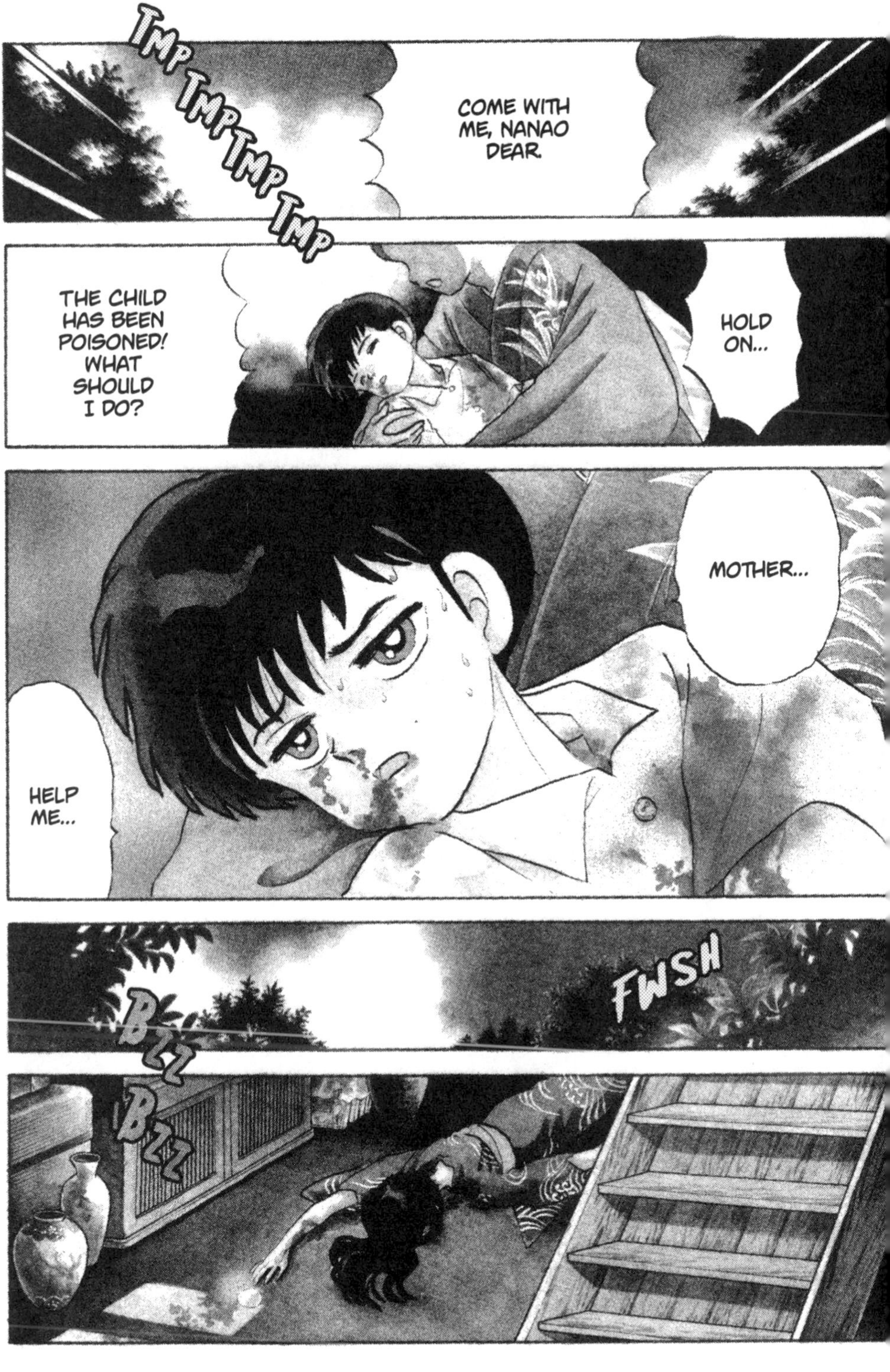
TMP TMP TMP TMP
COME WITH ME, NANAO DEAR.
HOLD ON...
THE CHILD HAS BEEN POISONED! WHAT SHOULD I DO?
MOTHER...
HELP ME...
FWSH
BZZ
BZZ

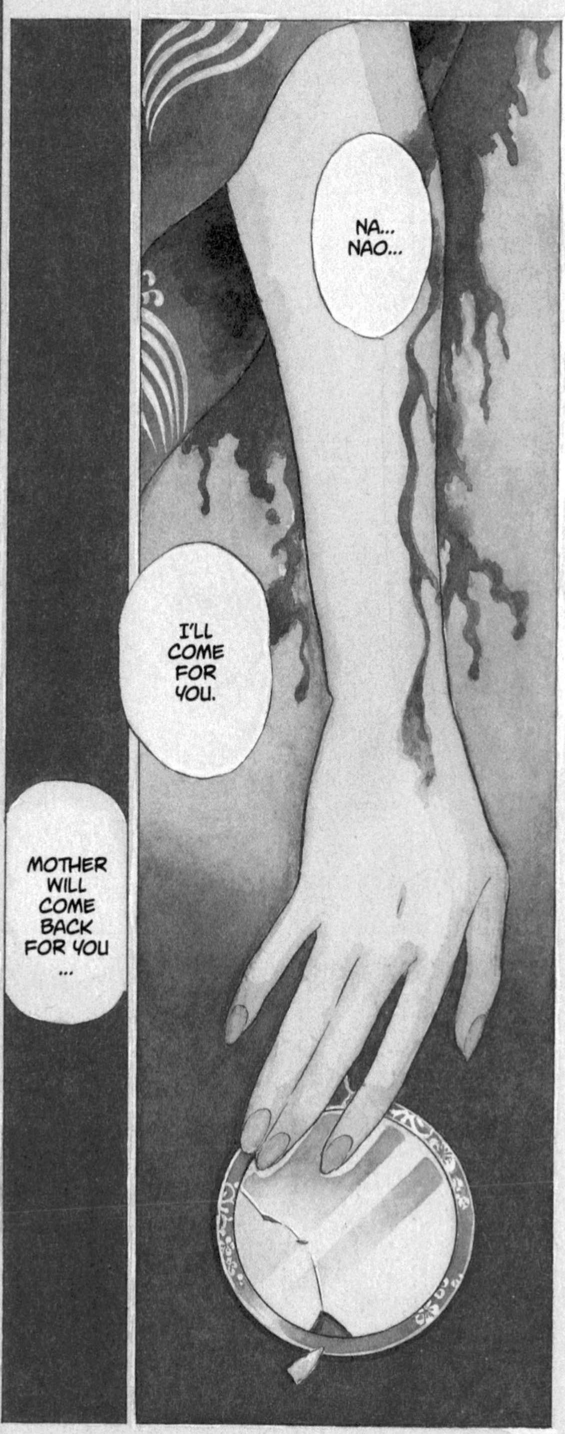
NA... NAO...
I'LL COME FOR YOU.
MOTHER WILL COME BACK FOR YOU ...

CHIRP CHIRP
UDON SOBA
UDON SOBA

Chapter 15: Mermaid's Mask, Part 1

VROOM
ARE YOU... HUNGRY?
I'VE GOT TO GO BACK...
...TO MY MOM.
TMP
I'M HOT. CAN I OPEN THE WINDOW?
ER... S-SURE.
FSH
!

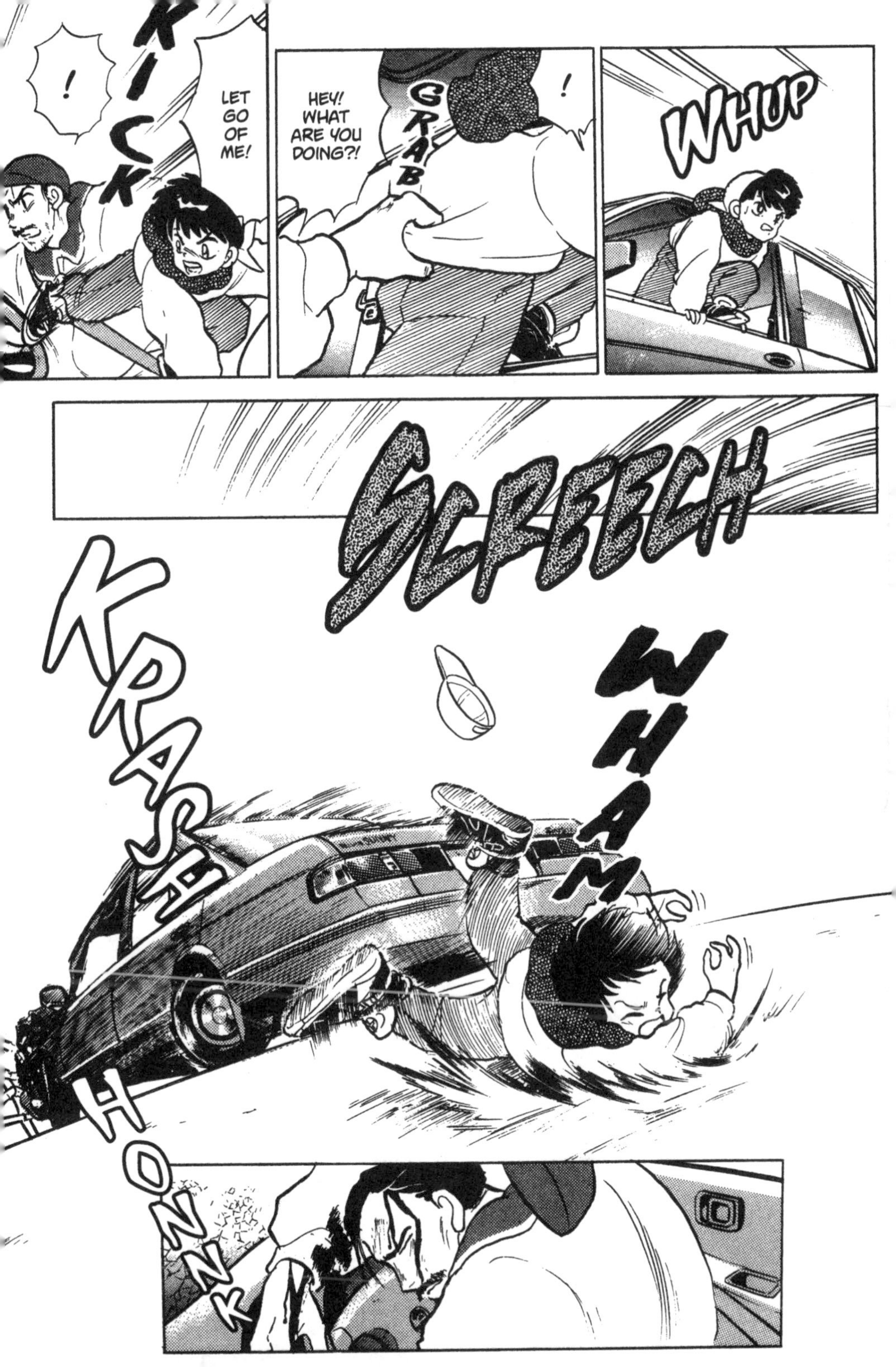
!
KICK
LET GO OF ME!
HEY! WHAT ARE YOU DOING?!
GRAB
!
WHUP
SCREECH
WHAM
KRASH
HONNK

...
UNH...
GRP
KLNK
SWAY
SPLSH
SPLSH
HFF.
HFF.
OWW...
SNFF

TMP
HEY, WHAT HAPPENED TO YOU, SQUIRT?
YOU'RE HURT!
IT'S ALL RIGHT.
I HAVE MEDI- CINE.
SHFF
GULP

WHEW.
SST
!
H- HEY!
GRAB
WHAT DID YOU JUST TAKE?!
L- LIKE I SAID...
IT'S OUR MEDICINE.

SHAA
FWSH
NANAO ...
NANAO, WHERE ARE YOU?

THAT'S ODD. WHERE COULD HE HAVE GONE THIS EARLY IN THE MORNING?
TMP
NANAO...
RUN, NANAO.
RUN AWAY.
YOU WERE KIDNAPPED?!
YEAH.
GRANDMA WOKE ME UP AT DAWN...
...AND TOLD ME TO GO WITH THIS MAN I NEVER SAW BEFORE.
SHE GAVE HIM THE BOX WITH THE ASHES IN IT TOO.
TAKE THIS ALSO.

AN URN? WHAT FOR?
WHAT'S IN IT?
ASHES, OF COURSE.
DASH
NANAO!
HFF HFF
THANK GOODNESS!
I WAS SO WORRIED ABOUT YOU!
MOM!
PHEW
NANAO, YOU LOOK LIKE YOU WERE HURT!
DID YOU TAKE YOUR MEDICINE LIKE YOU'RE SUPPOSED TO?
HELLO.

OUR MEDICINE?
YEAH.
ARE YOU THE ONE WHO GIVES IT TO HIM?
THAT'S NO ORDINARY MEDI-CINE...
...IS IT?
STRANGE, ISN'T IT?
NO, IT ISN'T.
IT'S BEEN IN OUR FAMILY FOR GENERA-TIONS.
IT CAN HEAL A MINOR WOUND JUST LIKE THAT!

ALL SHE HAS TO SAY IS, "STRANGE, ISN'T IT?"
WHAT DO YOU THINK, MANA?
IT MAY COME FROM A MERMAID.
SHK
NANAO MUSTN'T STAY IN THIS HOUSE.
WHY DID YOU BRING HIM BACK?
YOU'RE SAYING WE SHOULDN'T HAVE?
TMP

THIS IS NANAO... AND HIS MOTHER...
A DIFFERENT WOMAN?
THIS CHILD TOO.
HE LOOKS LIKE NANAO, BUT HE ISN'T HIM.
GRANDMA, WHAT ARE YOU DOING TALKING SUCH NONSENSE TO STRANGERS?
PLEASE EXCUSE HER.
SO LONG!

...
YUTA...
IS...
...THAT SQUIRT ONE OF US?
I DON'T KNOW.
BUT...
...WE CAN'T JUST WALK AWAY.
GOSSIP ABOUT THE HOUSE WITH THE OLD STORAGE SHED?
SURE, THERE'S GOSSIP!
THE MOTHER WAS DIVORCED FROM THE PRESIDENT OF SOME COMPANY, YOU SEE, AND–
AH!
NOT THAT KIND OF GOSSIP!
DISHES
THANK YOU FOR
WELL, WHEN THEY WERE FIGHTING OVER THEIR ONLY SON, THERE WAS A BLOODY INCIDENT.
OH YEAH?

THE MOTHER ABSOLUTELY DOTED ON THE BOY...
...AND APPARENTLY DECIDED SHE'D RATHER DIE THAN LOSE HIM, SO SHE DRAGGED THE BOY INTO THE STOREHOUSE...
...AND FED HIM **POISON**.
POI-SON?!
THE BOY ENDED UP BEING TAKEN AWAY BY THE MAN'S NEW WIFE. SHE WAS THE ONE WHO HAPPENED TO FIND THEM...
...AND THEY SAY THE MOTHER WAS LEFT WITH A HORRIBLE SCAR ON HER FACE.
BUT THIS ALL HAPPENED 25 YEARS AGO.
I FORGET THE SON'S NAME...
...BUT HE WAS A CLASSMATE OF MINE IN ELEMENTARY SCHOOL.
FISH SPECIAL
TOFU
MISO
BEEF
FIRE

ANYWAY, THEY'RE GONE NOW.
SOMEONE ELSE LIVES IN THAT HOUSE.
FWOO

SHHHK
FWMP
RUSTLE

FWOOO
RTTL
SHHK
NANAO ...

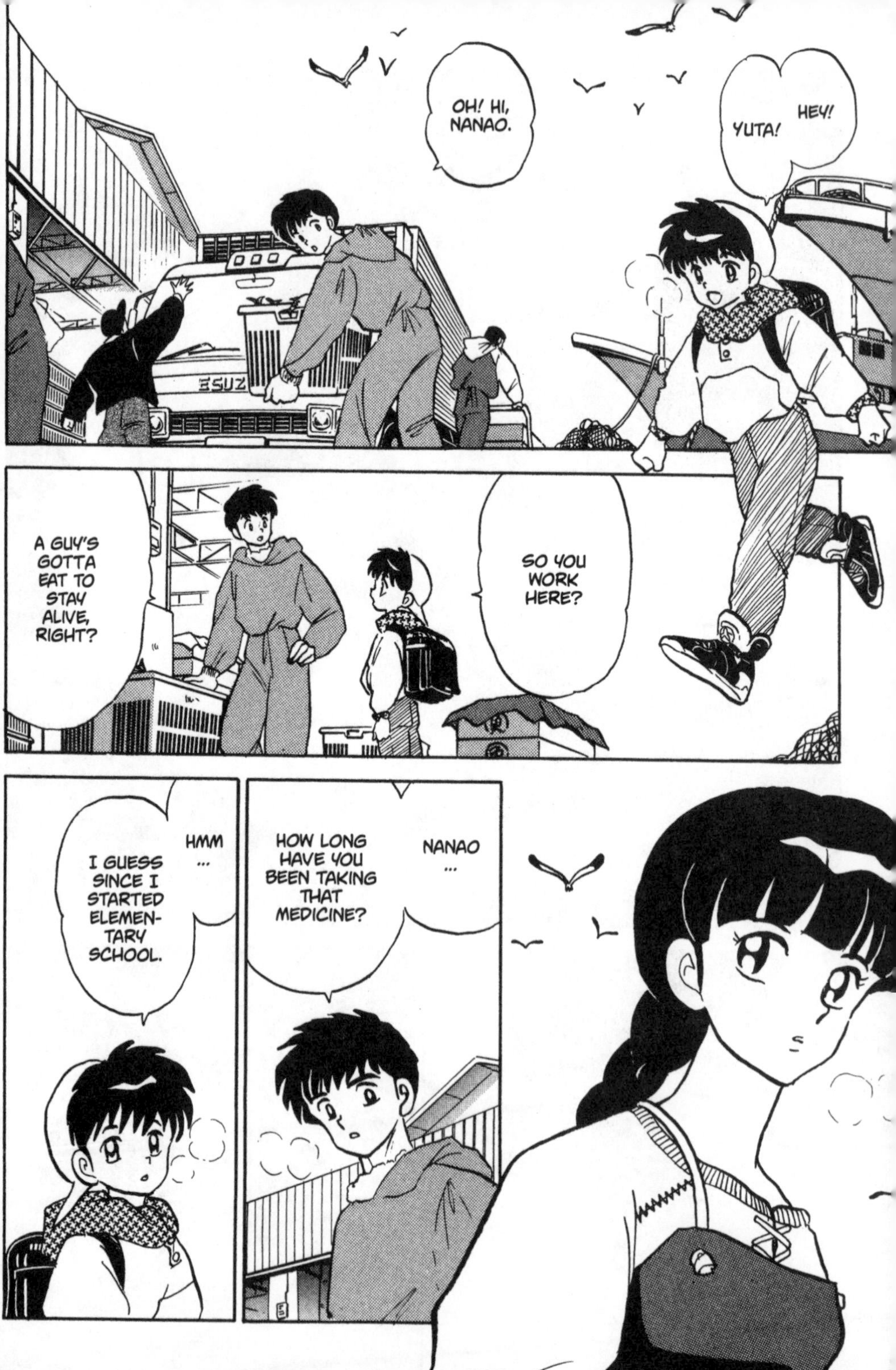
HEY! YUTA!
OH! HI, NANAO.
ESUZ
SO YOU WORK HERE?
A GUY'S GOTTA EAT TO STAY ALIVE, RIGHT?
NANAO ...
HOW LONG HAVE YOU BEEN TAKING THAT MEDICINE?
HMM ...
I GUESS SINCE I STARTED ELEMENTARY SCHOOL.

WHEN I WAS LITTLE, IT USED TO MAKE ME SPIT UP BLOOD.
WHAT ?!
BUT SHE KEPT GIVING IT TO YOU ANYWAY?!
WHAT KIND OF MOTHER IS SHE?!
PROMISE ME SOME-THING, NANAO.
PROMISE YOU'LL NEVER TAKE THAT MEDICINE AGAIN, EVEN IF YOUR MOTHER GIVES IT TO YOU.
WELL?
WHAP
OKAY.
GOOD.
HEY! THAT'S HIM!
LONGSHOREMEN'S UNION

THAT'S THE GUY WHO KIDNAPPED ME!
FWP
YUTA...
I'M GOING TO TALK TO HIM.
TMP
I HEARD YOU TRIED TO DRIVE OFF WITH THIS BOY WITHOUT TELLING HIS MOTHER!
WHY?
...
THAT BOY'S MOTHER ...
...
HEY...
SWAY
MANA, YOU TAKE NANAO HOME.
I'M GOING TO FOLLOW THAT GUY.
TABAC
IT'S ME.

...
FWOO
MANA ...
WILL YUTA BE ALL RIGHT?
DON'T WORRY, YUTA CAN TAKE CARE OF HIMSELF.
MOM?
TMP

KREE
...?
FWOO
SHE'S BEEN IN THERE PRETTY LONG. WHAT'S SHE DOING?
I'M NOT SURE ...
SHE TOLD ME NEVER TO GO IN THE STOREHOUSE.
KREE
KREEEEE
?!

JUMP
SHE LOOKS LIKE...
THIS IS NANAO... AND HIS MOTHER...
...THE WOMAN IN THAT PHOTOGRAPH...
WHO'S THAT?
I DON'T KNOW.
SHF

SHAA
SHAA
IS HE WAITING FOR SOMEONE?
!
TMP

SHAA
WHO'S THAT WOMAN?
NANAO ...
YOU ARE NANAO, AREN'T YOU?
NANAO?!

MOTHER...
FOOSH
?!
IS IT REALLY YOU, MOTHER?
THAT'S RIGHT, NANAO.
THOSE TWO ARE MOTHER AND CHILD?!
THAT'S CRAZY! SHE'S TOO YOUNG...!

LOOK AT THIS.
I'VE TREASURED THIS MIRROR ALL THESE YEARS.
AFTER ALL, IT WAS A PRESENT FROM YOU.
YOU SAVED YOUR MEAGER ALLOWANCE FOR MONTHS TO BUY THIS FOR ME.
IT MADE ME SO HAPPY.
MOTHER...
LET ME HAVE NANAO...
LET ME HAVE MY SON BACK!
!

!
W
OOSH
DASH
WHAT THE HELL ARE YOU DOING?!
JUST WHO THE HELL ARE-
WHUP

FSH
!
THAT SCAR...
SHIK
!
SHAK

SLUMP
KSHH
UNH...
SKRKK
H- HEY...
HANG IN THERE!
NANA... O...
THE NANAO THAT WOMAN IS RAISING...
...IS MY SON.
MINE.

THAT WOMAN...
SHE'S EATEN THE FLESH OF A MERMAID, HASN'T SHE?
I HAVE TOO. THAT'S HOW I CAN TELL.
THAT SCAR ON HER FACE WAS CAUSED BY THE MERMAID'S POISON.
TWENTY-FIVE YEARS AGO, MY MOTHER AND I BOTH ATE MERMAID FLESH.
TWENTY-FIVE YEARS AGO? THAT'S WHEN THE INCIDENT OCCURRED AT THAT HOUSE.
SHE FORCED ME TO EAT IT.
IT STUNG AS IF IT WERE ON FIRE. I THREW IT UP RIGHT AWAY.
EVEN SO, I WAS LEFT WITH A SCAR THAT HAS NEVER GONE AWAY.
YOU TOO...?
BUT I'VE CONTINUED TO AGE NORMALLY.
SHE...

THE WOMAN I MET TODAY... HASN'T CHANGED SINCE THE DAY WE PARTED 25 YEARS AGO.
SHE LOOKS AS YOUNG NOW AS SHE WAS THEN.
EIGHT YEARS AGO, MY MOTHER SUDDENLY APPEARED.
SHE TOOK MY SON, WHO HAD JUST TURNED TWO.
THEN THEY DISAPPEARED.
I SEARCHED AND SEARCHED...

MY GRANDMOTHER CONTACTED ME AND TOLD ME MY MOTHER HAD RETURNED TO THE HOUSE.
...AND I FINALLY FOUND THEM.
SHE GAVE MY SON...
...THE SAME NAME SHE HAD GIVEN ME—NANAO.
YOU MEAN HE WAS JUST A SUBSTITUTE FOR YOU?
I DON'T KNOW.
I DON'T KNOW WHAT SHE MEANS TO DO WITH HIM.
IF THAT'S TRUE, THEN WHO IS THAT WOMAN...
...WHO CLAIMS TO BE NANAO'S MOTHER?!

FWOOO
WE SAW HER COME IN. SHE MUST BE IN HERE SOMEWHERE.
MOM? WHERE ARE YOU?
HMM?
THIS IS THE BLOUSE SHE WAS WEARING WHEN SHE CAME IN.

BLOOD ?!
SHUNK
BANDAGES COVERED WITH BLOOD...
WHAT...
...ON EARTH ...?
THIS BOX...
WHUP

A FACE...
A FRESHLY SKINNED HUMAN FACE!!
WHAT ARE YOU DOING, MANA?
TWITCH
GRAB
JOLT
MANA!!

Chapter 16:
Mermaid's Mask,
Part 2

MANA!!

FSH
KSHHH
!
MANA!!
TMP
S-STAY AWAY, NANAO!
RUN!
SHUP
FSH
KLAK

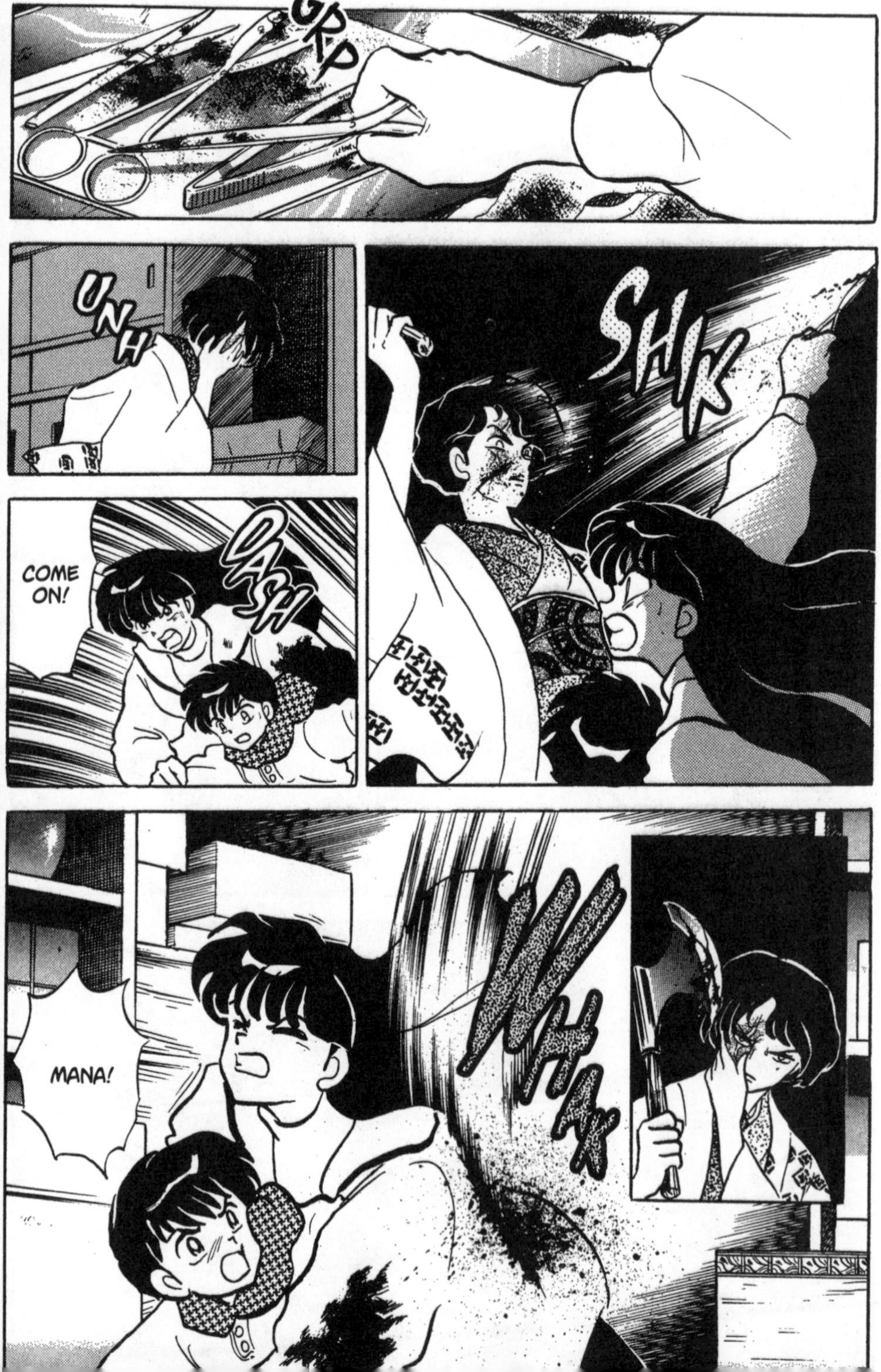
GRP
SHK
UNH
DASH
COME ON!
WHAK
MANA!

SWAY
SLUMP
UNH...
THROB
FWOO
HIDE HERE, MANA.
I'LL BRING MOTHER'S MEDICINE.
THERE'S SOME IN MY ROOM.
NO...
I DON'T NEED ANY MEDICINE ...
WAIT HERE!
DASH
NANAO ...
THAT MEDICINE...
...CAN CURE ANYTHING.

...
SKRSH
THAT FACE IN THE BOX...
A SKINNED HUMAN FACE...
I HAVE TO TELL YUTA!
FLUMP
FWOOO
SHK

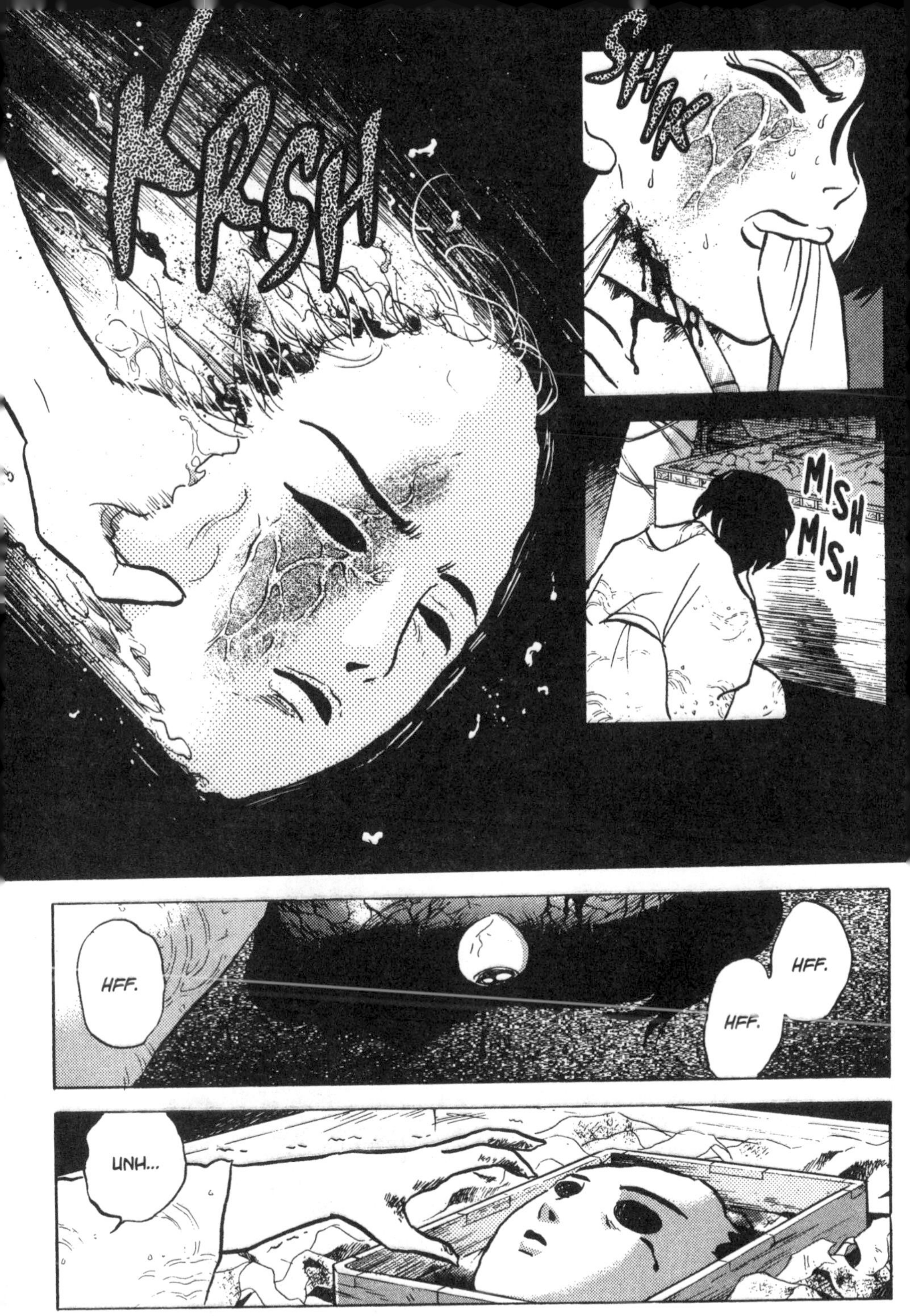
KRSH
SHNK
MISH MISH MISH
HFF.
HFF.
HFF.
UNH...

DRAG...
THERE'S THE WOMAN WHO ATE THE FLESH OF A MERMAID...
...AND KIDNAPPED NANAO WHEN HE WAS A BABY...
AND THERE'S THE WOMAN WHO IS RAISING NANAO...
...AND GIVING HIM A MEDICINE THAT CAN HEAL ANY WOUND.
THEY HAVE COMPLETELY DIFFERENT FACES...
...BUT COULD THEY BE THE SAME PERSON?

FWOOOO
HFF... HFF...
SHA
JOLT
NANA...O...
AH!
MOM!

MOM!
NANAO ...
MOM, YOU HAVE TO HELP.
SOME CRAZY WOMAN ATTACKED MANA-
HEY!
YOU'RE HURT TOO-!
I'M FINE.
EVERY-THING'S ALL RIGHT NOW, NANAO.
NANAO ...
WHERE IS THAT GIRL?
I'LL GO TAKE CARE OF HER.
YOU STAY RIGHT HERE, NANAO.
IS THAT CLEAR?
SKRK
TMP

SO...
YOU'RE STILL ALIVE.
WHAT IS THAT THING...
...IN THE STOREHOUSE?!
AH.
YOU DID SEE IT, THEN.
FWP
!
UNH...
DRAG
!
MANA!
YUTA...

SKRSH
HFF HFF
WHAT ARE YOU DOING TO MANA?!
YUTA!
YANK
UNH!
VSH

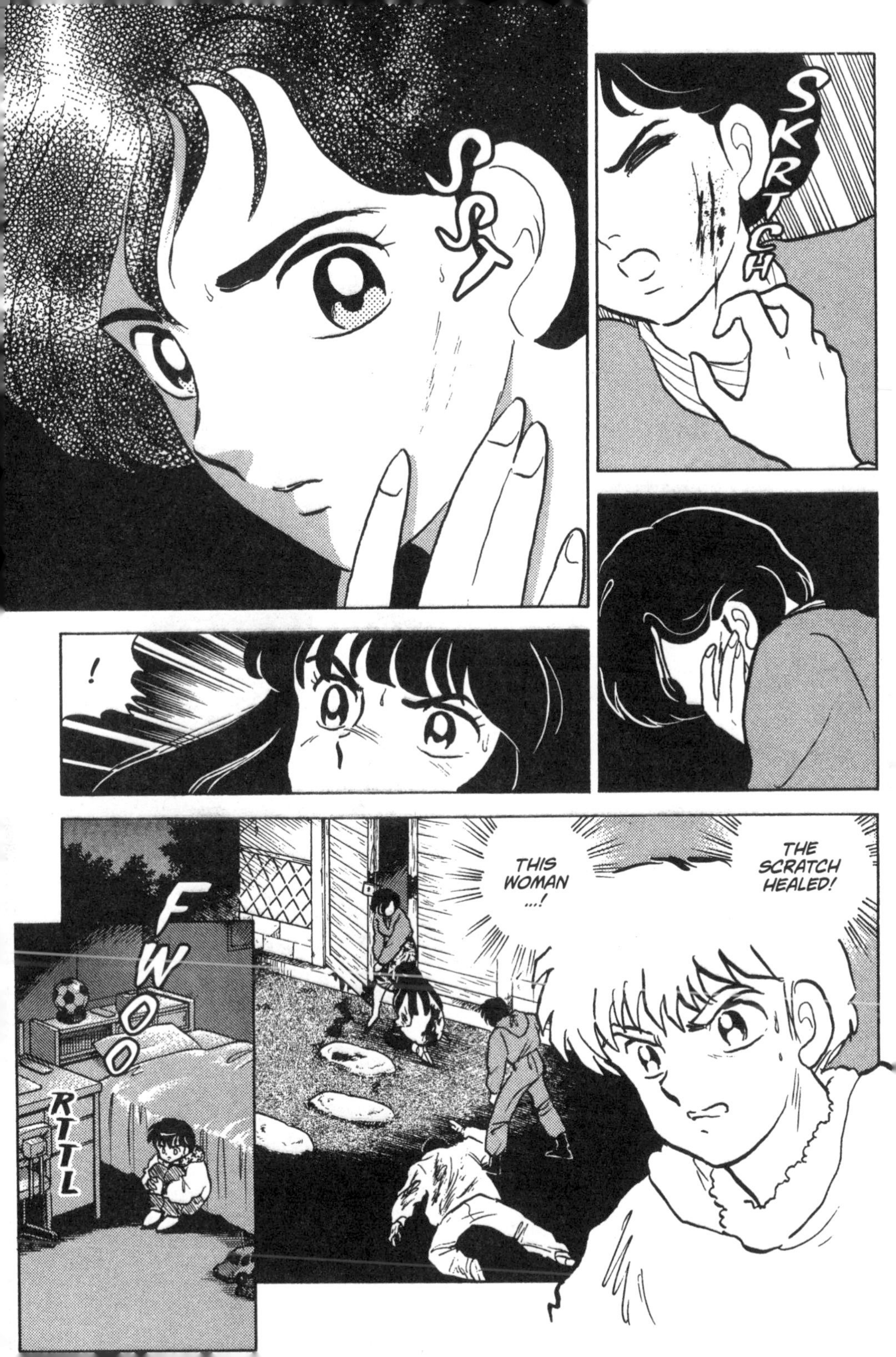
SKRTCH
!
THE SCRATCH HEALED!
THIS WOMAN ...!
FWOOO
RTTL

MOM TOLD ME TO STAY HERE...
...BUT THAT WOMAN MIGHT STILL BE AROUND.
I'VE GOT TO PROTECT HER!
SHFF
AH!
NANAO ...
GR...
GRANDMA ...
GIVE ME...
...THE MEDICINE ...
I-I CAN'T. I HAVE TO GIVE THIS TO MANA...
GIVE IT TO ME!

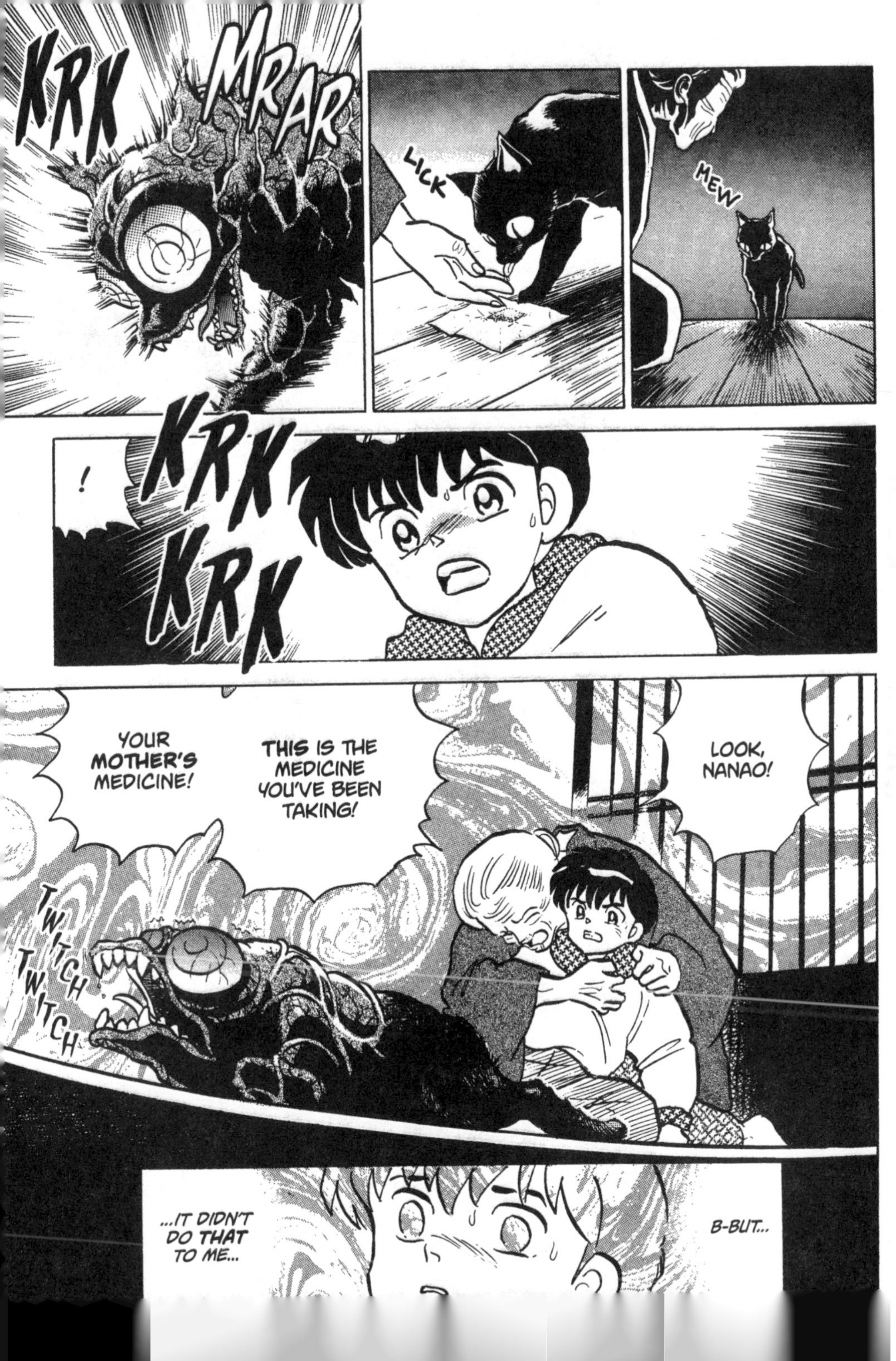
MEW
LICK
MRAR
KRK
!
KRK
KRK
KRK
LOOK, NANAO!
THIS IS THE MEDICINE YOU'VE BEEN TAKING!
YOUR MOTHER'S MEDICINE!
TWITCH
TWITCH
B-BUT...
...IT DIDN'T DO THAT TO ME...

YOU MUST ESCAPE, NANAO.
WHAT ARE YOU TALKING ABOUT, GRANDMA?!
THAT WOMAN IS NOT YOUR MOTHER.
WHA-?!
THAT WOMAN IS DANGEROUS.
YOU-
THAT'S NOT TRUE!
WHUP
YOU...
YOU'VE EATEN THE FLESH OF A MERMAID TOO!
WHO ARE YOU?
I...
...HAVE BEEN ALIVE FOR 500 YEARS.

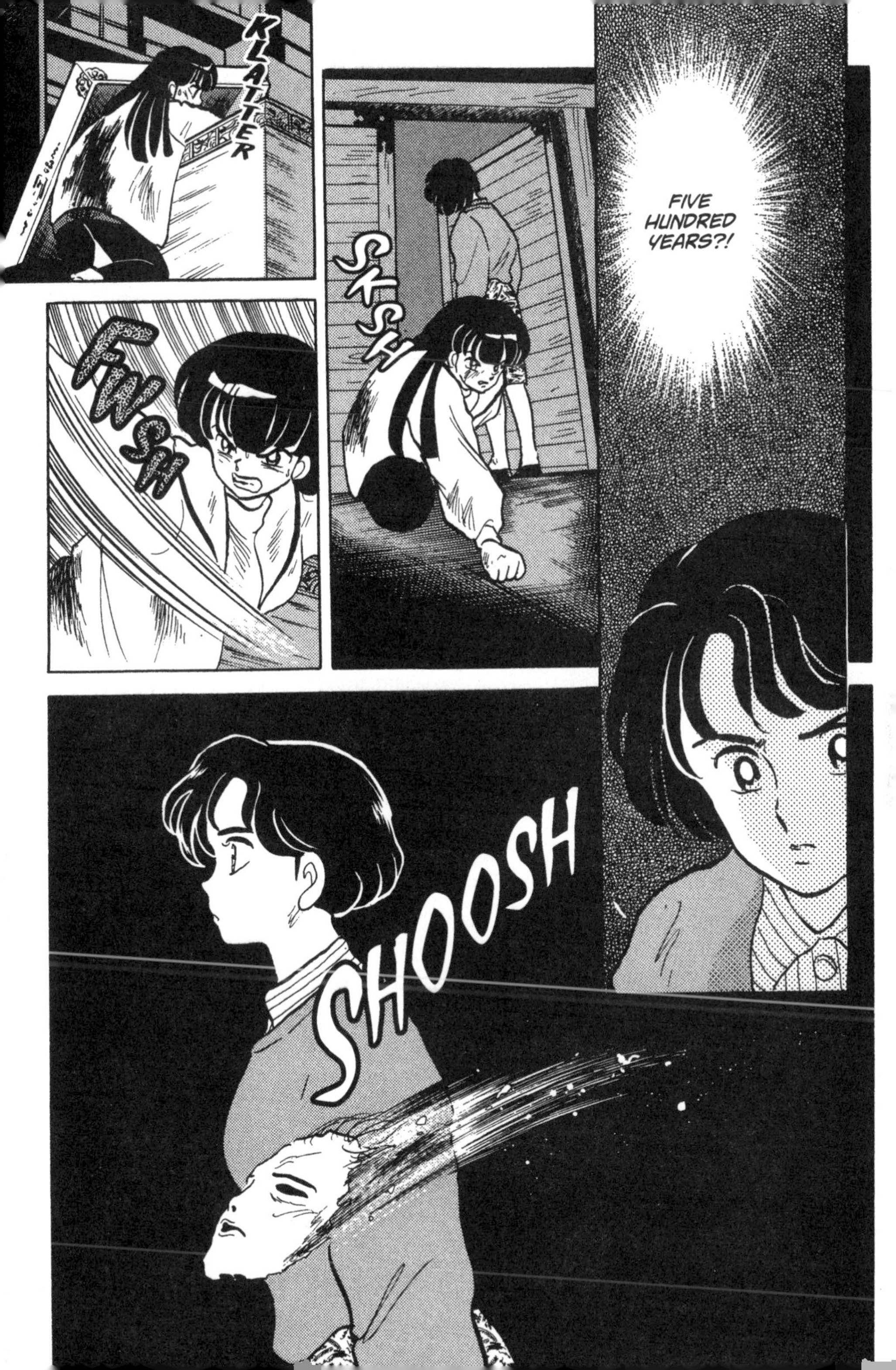
KLATTER
FWSH
SKSH
FIVE HUNDRED YEARS?!
SHOOSH

!
THUP
THAT SCAR...
IT'S THE SAME AS...!

YOU...
...CHANGED FACES?
...?
WEREN'T YOU SCARRED AT ALL?
DIDN'T IT HURT?
TWENTY-FIVE YEARS AGO...
...THE FATHER OF THIS NANAO WAS THREATENING TO TAKE HIM AWAY FROM ME.
MOTHER ...?
HE WAS MY WHOLE LIFE.
"MOTHER, I'M GOING TO GO WITH FATHER."

I DECIDED I'D RATHER HAVE HIM DIE WITH ME THAN LOSE HIM.
I FED HIM POISON.
BUT IN THE END, WE WERE SEPARATED ANYWAY.
AS FOR ME...
...THE MERMAID'S POISON LEFT ME IN PAIN.
THE PAIN BECAME WORSE WITH EACH PASSING YEAR.
DID YOU KNOW, NANAO...
...THAT I USED TO COME SEE YOU ONCE IN A WHILE?

YOU GREW UP...
...AND HAD A BABY.
HE WAS SO CUTE. IT WAS AS IF YOU HAD COME BACK TO ME.
MOTHER!
THAT CHILD ISN'T ME!
IT WAS RIGHT AFTER I TOOK HIM AWAY...
...THAT I FOUND THIS FACE.
SHE WAS DEAD.
WASHED UP ON THE SHORE.
WHEN I PUT ON HER FACE, THE PAIN VANISHED.
MOM!
NANAO...
!

AH!
NANAO...
SKSH
COME HERE, NANAO!
!
I'M YOUR FATHER, NANAO!
I'VE COME TO RESCUE YOU!
...
COME HERE, NANAO.
MOM...
TMP

THUK
STAY BACK, NANAO!
FWP
AH...
W-WAIT!
WHAT ARE YOU GOING TO–?!
GRAB
IT'S ALL RIGHT.
HE WON'T DIE.

I PLANNED TO DO THIS WHEN YOU WERE A BIT OLDER, BUT...
YOU DON'T MEAN TO FEED HIM MERMAID FLESH–?!
!

DON'T DO IT!
YOU KNOW IT'S POISON!
HE'LL BE FINE.
I GROUND THE MERMAID FLESH INTO POWDER...
...AND GAVE IT TO HIM BIT BY BIT TO BUILD UP HIS TOLERANCE.
!
YOU WHAT?!

DAMN YOU!
TMP
KREEE
BAM
ONLY ONE IN A THOUSAND PEOPLE CAN BECOME COMPLETELY IMMORTAL!
TUMP
TUMP
DON'T YOU GET IT?!
SKSH
WHAT ARE YOU LOOKING FOR?
THE MERMAID FLESH?

!
NANAO-!
TUMP
TUMP
DAMMIT.
STAGGER
NGH!
GRP
VSH
INCRED-IBLE.
YOUR WOUND HAS ALMOST HEALED.

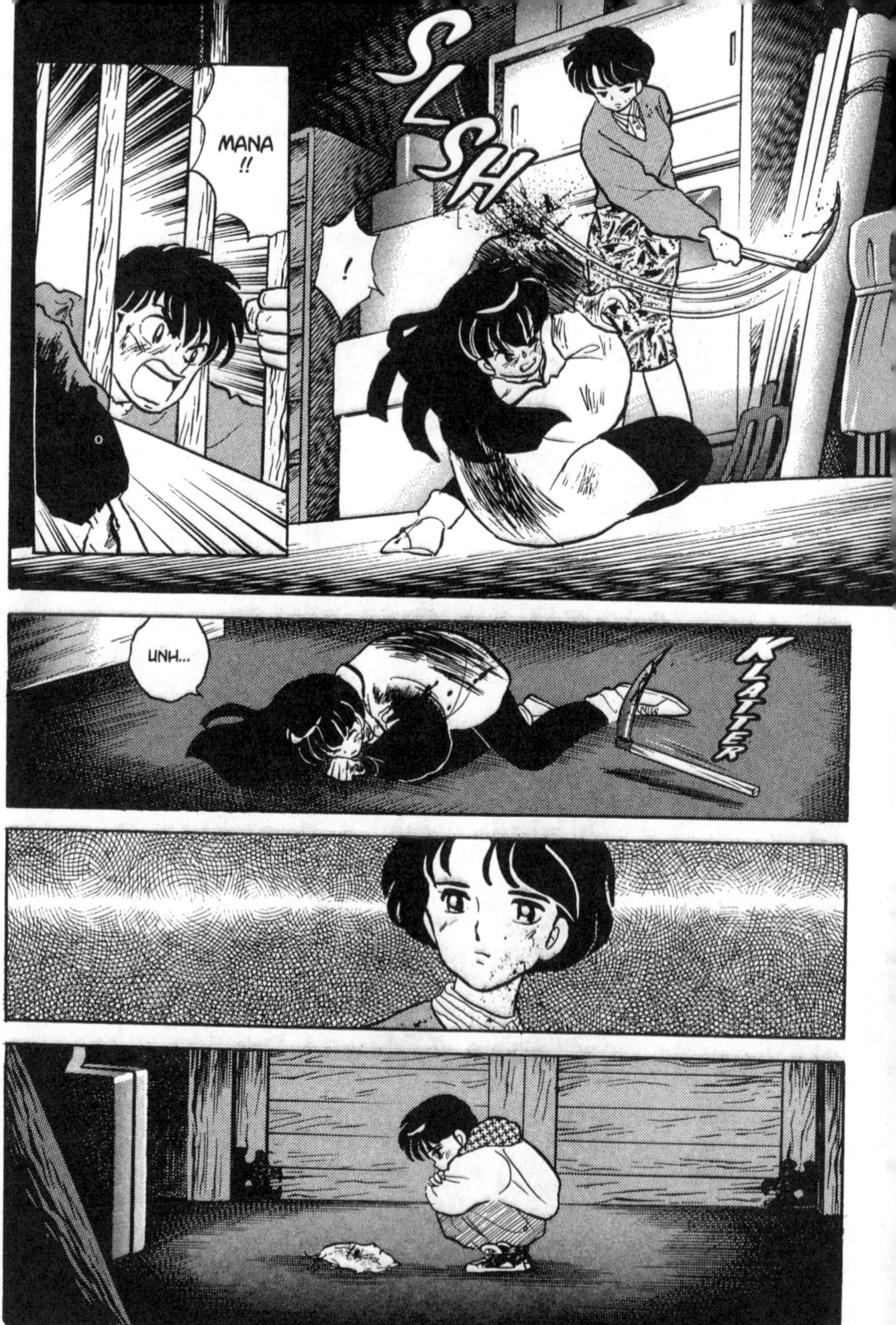
SLSH
MANA !!
!
UNH...
KLATTER

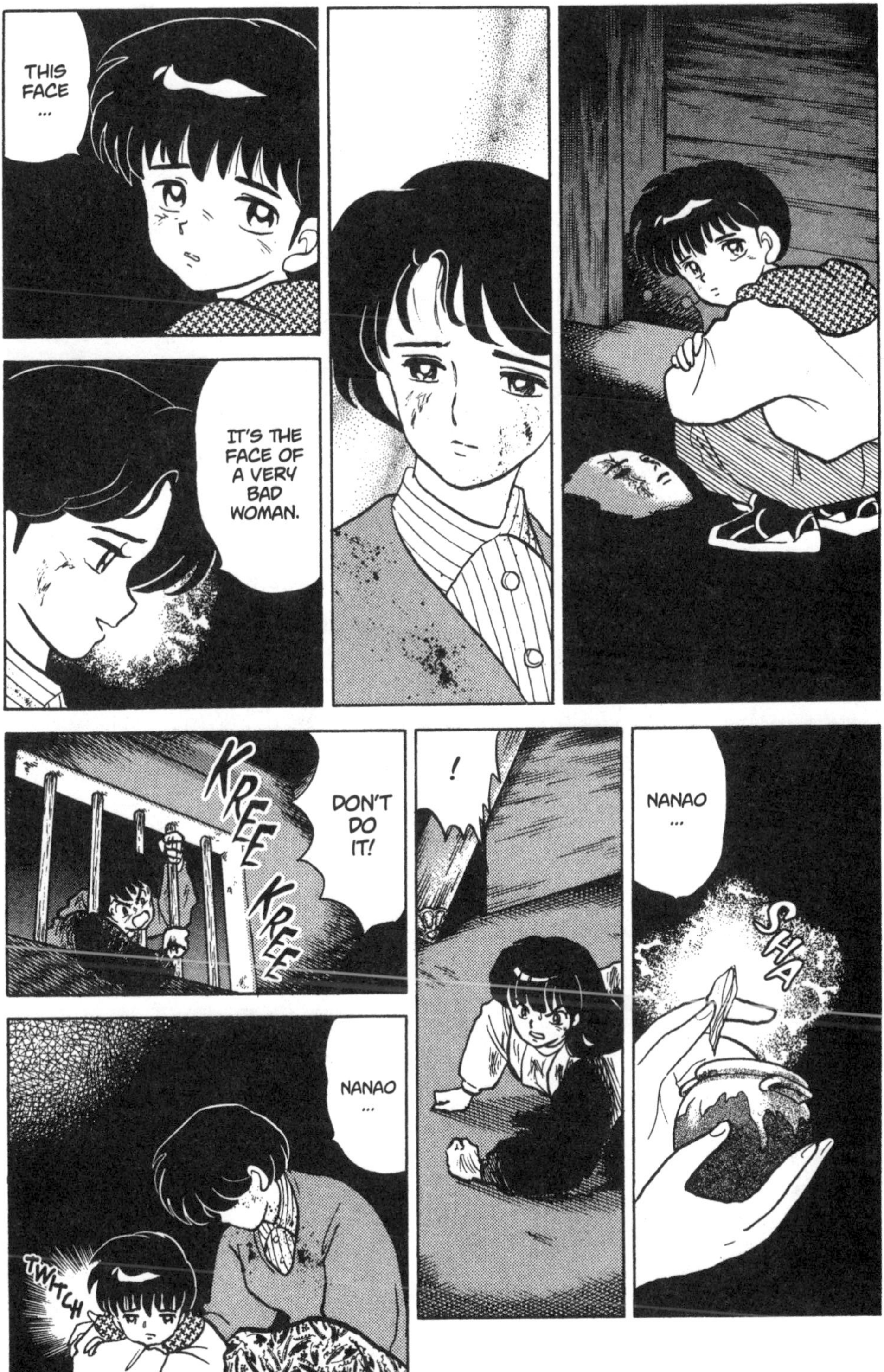
THIS FACE ...
IT'S THE FACE OF A VERY BAD WOMAN.
NANAO ...
SHA
!
DON'T DO IT!
KREE KREE
NANAO ...
TWITCH

WELL, NANAO?
WILL YOU EAT THIS FOR ME?
ARE...
ARE YOU REALLY MY MOM?
YES.
YOUR MOTHER ...
...HAS EATEN THIS TOO.
IT'S NOT POISON.

!
SHATTER!

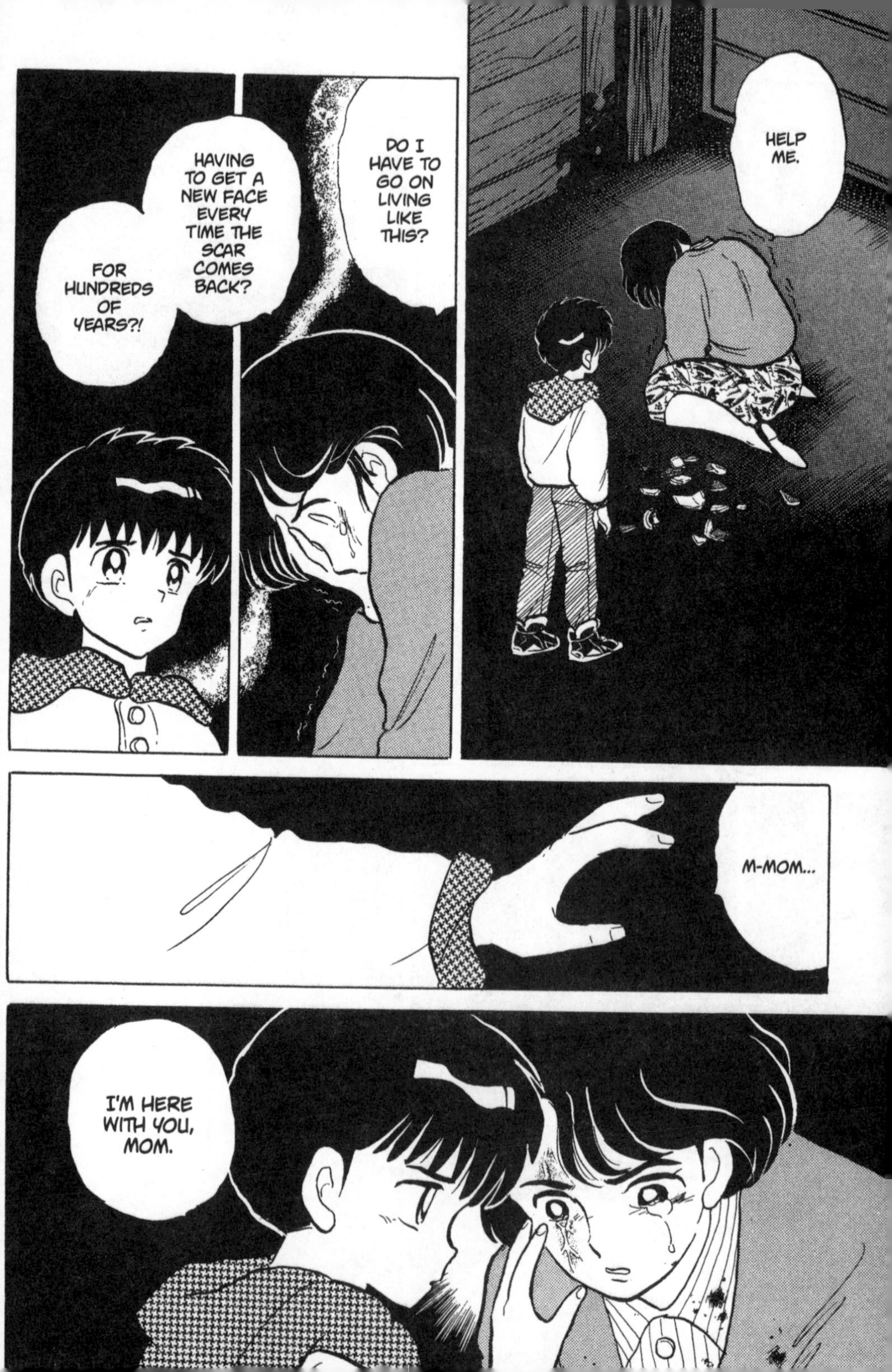

HELP ME.
DO I HAVE TO GO ON LIVING LIKE THIS?
HAVING TO GET A NEW FACE EVERY TIME THE SCAR COMES BACK?
FOR HUNDREDS OF YEARS?!
M-MOM...
I'M HERE WITH YOU, MOM.

I'LL EAT IT.
NANAO...!
I MEAN...
IT WON'T HURT ME, RIGHT?
YOU FOOL!

IT MIGHT BE POISONOUS.
EAT IT, NANAO!
NO!
NO, MOTHER!
IT MIGHT NOT WORK THIS TIME EITHER.
BUT...
CLENCH

KRASH
IMP
DON'T EAT IT!
WHAP
TUP

YOU'RE 100 YEARS TOO YOUNG ...
...TO DO SOME-THING LIKE THAT.
...
YOU SHOULD HAVE BEEN THE ONE TO STOP HIM.
I... I'M TOO WEAK FOR THAT.

SWAY
TMP
...
I'M GIVING THIS BACK TO YOU.
HERE.
ALONG WITH HIM.
MOTHER ...

MOM...
NANAO. YOUR MOTHER ...
...IS GOING TO GO SOME-PLACE FAR AWAY.
MOM...?!
TMP
YUTA.
DO YOU THINK...?
...
THERE WAS A MYSTERIOUS FIRE IN ONE OF THE WARE-HOUSES AT THE HARBOR.
SHA
THEY FOUND ONE BODY.
A WOMAN, APPAR-ENTLY.

HMM.
SO YOUR MOM WON'T BE COMING BACK?
SHA
NOPE.
I'M GONNA BE LIVING WITH THAT GUY.
TOK
I WONDER WHERE SHE WENT.
MOM ...
...
WELL, I CAN SEE WHY YOU'D FEEL LONELY.
YOU'RE JUST A LITTLE SQUIRT, AFTER ALL.

Mermaid's Mask / The End

Rumiko Takahashi

The spotlight on Rumiko Takahashi's career began in 1978 when she won an honorable mention in Shogakukan's prestigious New Comic Artist Contest for *Those Selfish Aliens*. Later that same year, her boy-meets-alien comedy series, *Urusei Yatsura*, was serialized in *Weekly Shonen Sunday*. This phenomenally successful manga series was adapted into anime format and spawned a TV series and half a dozen theatrical-release movies, all incredibly popular in their own right. Takahashi followed up the success of her debut series with one blockbuster hit after another—*Maison Ikkoku* ran from 1980 to 1987, *Ranma 1/2* from 1987 to 1996, and *Inuyasha* from 1996 to 2008. Other notable works include *Mermaid Saga*, *Rumic Theater*, and *One-Pound Gospel*.

Takahashi was inducted into the Will Eisner Comic Awards Hall of Fame in 2018. In 2019, she won the Grand Prix at FIDB Angoulême. She won the prestigious Shogakukan Manga Award twice in her career, once for *Urusei Yatsura* in 1981 and the second time for *Inuyasha* in 2002. A majority of the Takahashi canon has been adapted into other media such as anime, live-action TV series, and film. Takahashi's manga, as well as the other formats her work has been adapted into, have continued to delight generations of fans around the world. Distinguished by her wonderfully endearing characters, Takahashi's work adeptly incorporates a wide variety of elements such as comedy, romance, fantasy, and martial arts. While her series are difficult to pin down into one simple genre, the signature style she has created has come to be known as the "Rumic World." Rumiko Takahashi is an artist who truly represents the very best from the world of manga.